M000309856

Journeying with the Poor

Raineer Chu

Urban Loft Publishers | Skyforest, CA

Journeying with the Poor

Copyright © 2019 Raineer Chu

All rights reserved. Except for brief quotations in critical publications or reviews, no part of this book may be reproduced in any manner without prior written permission from the publisher.
Write: Permissions, Urban Loft Publishers
Skyforest, CA 92385

Senior Editors: Stephen Burris & Kendi Howells Douglas
Copy Editor: Christian Arnold
Graphics: Amber Craft

Unless otherwise indicated, all Scripture quotations are from The Holy Bible, English Standard Version, copyright © 2001 by Crossway Bibles, a division of Good News Publishers. Used by permission. All rights reserved.

Some names and exact locations have been changed for those who desire to remain anonymous.

ISBN-13: 978-1-949625-01-1

Made in the U.S.

*All they asked was that we should continue
to remember the poor,
the very thing I had been eager to do all along.*
Galatians 2:10

By Companion With the Poor

*Collected, written, narrated, and edited by
Raineer Chu, Paul Rollet and Ariel Lev Pinzon.
With special thanks to the many people who
have read this book in its earlier stages,
and provided important feedback.*

*This is our story,
a story about community, solitude and the poor.*

TABLE OF CONTENTS

They devoted themselves to the apostles' teaching and to fellowship, to the breaking of bread and to prayer. Everyone was filled with awe at the many wonders and signs performed by the apostles. All the believers were together and had everything in common. They sold property and possessions to give to anyone who had need. Every day they continued to meet together in the temple courts. They broke bread in their homes and ate together with glad and sincere hearts, praising God and enjoying the favor of all the people. And the Lord added to their number daily those who were being saved.
– Acts 2:42-47

Author's Preface

I am not saying this because I am in need, for I have learned to be content whatever the circumstances. I know what it is to be in need, and I know what it is to have plenty. I have learned the secret of being content in any and every situation, whether well fed or hungry, whether living in plenty or in want. I can do all things through him who gives me strength. – Philippians 4:11-13

Whenever I bring my students to the slums, I give them only one instruction: to find out what they can live without. When they sleep in the slums, will they be able to survive without their bed or their toothpaste or their toilet paper? The moment they say they cannot live without one thing or another, their journey with the poor stops.

In our journey with the poor, we are confronted with material objects we are attached to. We are challenged to ask, what is it we cannot live without? Our goal is not to turn students into rigid stoics, or Spartans who reject luxuries or extravagance. The goal is to find our freedom.

The Apostle Paul said, "I know what it is to live in plenty and I know what it is to live in want" (Philippians 4:11). When we are bound by our material possessions, we have no freedom. As Christians, we must be able to say that even without our laptop or cell phone, we will survive. I can enjoy the lavish life of the wealthy but I also will not be crippled when cast into utter poverty.

Later, a student asked me, "How do I draw the line? How do I know I am no longer too extreme, excessive, and abnormal?" I believe the line is found in our freedom. All Christians have this freedom. It was for freedom that God has called us. And it was in this freedom that Jesus, though he was rich, made himself poor in order to make others rich.

Introduction

There are many elements in this book that supply some of the missing components in many evangelical books about social action. One is a good and solid theology of church as the central instrument in the plan of redemption, not just an add-on to the many Christian transformational ministries.

Another is the need to balance the exclusively top-down developmental approach to poverty alleviation. Transformation or development needs to be balanced with a strong contemplative approach. It requires a spiritual journey aimed at seeing how and why the Bible says the poor are rich in faith. It is also to be able to gain the spiritual insight taught by Mother Teresa from where we can see Christ in the dying, in the sick and in the poor.

We have promoted an ideal future based on justice and deliverance texts from Scripture, but these have no link with the church (ecclesiology), or the anguished hope of the believers—especially the poor (eschatology), and salvation (soteriology). We know that the gospel, church and kingdom should never be separate from the other. We must be critical of proof-text approaches to the Bible or using single passages to support a theological argument. Instead, we must seek the integrated approach, the one that makes sense of the Scripture in its entirety, not in partiality. A good hermeneutic is one that gives the most meaning to the entire Bible taken together.

The church should be central to the plan of redemption. God's plan to transform the world cannot take place without

His Covenant people. Christians cannot work in an individualistic way; we cannot be disorganized and be called the Body of Christ at the same time. Upholding God's covenant as His people means having a community. It is not having a professional model where the poor of the world are only given their needs and then left alone. This is the model promoted by a lot of NGOs, where, in the end, they separate themselves from the world's poor.

The church has only one mission, and that is to evangelize. The end goal is for all peoples to come to know salvation through Christ. There is no pressure to balance evangelism with social action. Social action is done within the community of believers, which is a step after evangelism. There is a conflict between the system that God intends for the cosmos, and the evil in discord with what is good.

God has no miraculous agenda to get rid of the poverty in the world at large. His agenda, following a structure taught by the Bible, is to get rid of poverty in the church. This is why the church is called the "contrast society". It is a counter-cultural community composed of believers who demonstrate living in the kingdom as the ideal life of shalom under the Lordship of God. One manifestation of this is that in the church there is no more poor. The social action to alleviate poverty must begin within the church as proof that our gospel works. It can overflow to the world at large but only after it has been shown to work within.

Without a community, we can have no ministry. Without community, there is no line drawn for unbelievers to cross over. They cannot genuinely show their allegiance to Jesus, as an act of defiance against the world. The gospel is not just about being saved to Jesus, it also means becoming part of a community, the people of God.

Part 1: Community

1: Begin with Community

It is our membership in community that qualifies us and enables us to serve in the ministry. Without community, we cannot preach the Gospel because there is no community that the new believer can join.

The first thing we need to do in journeying with the poor is understand community.

My journey with the poor had many beginnings. The first was among the street children in Cubao, Quezon City. I was a staff member with Navigators at the University of the Philippines. Every weekend from 10:00pm to 2:00am, we ministered to the kids. We were very encouraged at the beginning, and we had many volunteers assisting us. We met with the street children and had them cleaned with a face towel and rubbing alcohol. There was hardly any tap water around.

We shared home-cooked meals while discussing the gospel, sang together and had lessons in reading and writing. Most of the children were illiterate, abused, and displaced from their homes. In the end, we decided with heavy hearts to abandon the ministry. We were very discouraged with the results. The success rate among the street children was almost negligible. The moment a child tastes the freedom of the streets, he is almost incorrigible. Out of a hundred kids we rescued in a year, only one or two eventually got out of the streets. It's almost similar with rehabilitating prostitutes or working with prison inmates. It was dismal.

My second journey began upon the invitation of a good friend. Viv Grigg, who then was starting a ministry that would span the entire globe, urged me to join him in the slums. It was 1979 in Tatalon, Quezon City. Viv barely ate anything while we worked in the slums, and the work was very exhausting. I remember having a hard time adjusting, coming home extremely tired and falling asleep on the floor even without dinner. At night, we stayed in a small cardboard shack, fit only for a few people. This was how we did ministry every day, no matter how exhausting it became at night. I ran away from Tatalon after a week. Beyond the exhaustion that never ended, it depressed me so much. But I never forgot my experiences there. My memories lingered on—everything I saw, heard, and even smelled. They all lingered like a virus taking its effect until I was fully contaminated.

A few years later, I ventured back into working with slum families. I joined an organization of Filipino and American missionaries called International Teams. I was assigned to the Payatas dumpsite, with all warnings of toxic and hospital waste, as well as deadly chemicals. Despite all that, I was very encouraged because of the progress we had.

So many flies infested the community that sometimes we couldn't see plants, trees or electric wires without flies. We had this joke in the dumpsite. When we began there, we were all die-hard Pentecostals. We sang at the top of our lungs until one of our song leaders swallowed a fly during the service. After that, we all became Baptists; we didn't move and hardly opened our mouths when we sang. This was the first time I felt part of a community of missionaries journeying together.

After serving with International Teams for ten years, some of us were introduced to Mission Ministries Philippines, Inc (MMP). MMP was also located in the slums and had multiple ministries, but their main focus was Christian preschools. Their leaders shared their desire to strengthen the church planting aspect of their ministry. When we finally decided to join MMP, our church planting team neither had money nor an office, but we felt called to partner with MMP in this new endeavor. By God's grace, over the last 20 years, both the preschool department and our church planting department have expanded ten-fold. We are able to plant four to five churches a year, and the preschool team continues to train and establish new preschools at an increasing rate. Between the church planting team and the preschool team, we now have over fifty full-time missionaries.

In 2014, our church planting team felt led to launch a new organization, that we called Companion With the Poor (CWTP). Though the preschool department continues to work as MMP, this change allows our church planting department to focus more on holistic church planting as our primary response to working with the poor, and to one day send workers to non-Christian nations like Indonesia, India, and countries in the Middle East. This change has also allowed our church planting community to restructure more like a religious community than a mission organization, which gives us the ability to balance our ministry with a liturgy and rule (or way) of life.

While we are still working out our rule of life as a community, we have already agreed upon many disciplines, or practices, that guide us as a community. The most important discipline is the Communion or Eucharist. Since we see the Eucharist or Communion as the heart of our prayer, our personal discipline is the frequent participation in this Sacrament. The second discipline is personal prayer. We set aside a definite time for prayer each day to spend time with God, to pray for others, and to express our thankfulness. The third discipline is to practice retreats. Silent retreats provide an opportunity to rest and grow physically, mentally and spiritually. At least three times a year, we participate in organized silent retreats.

The fourth discipline is studying about and for the Gospel. CWTP assists people academically, helping them get degrees and certificates suited for their ministry. The fifth is simplicity of living. We are called to a life of simplicity, eliminating our preoccupations with belongings that prevent our full expression of God's love. Lastly, the sixth discipline is obedience. All of our staff members are obedient to the decisions of our leadership council, and support each other by prayer, attendance at CWTP events, and contribution of financial support.

Members go through their journey to becoming part of our community. The first is a two-year exposure where the candidate sees if we are really his or her community, as well as for the leaders to help the candidate get adjusted in the community. They become part of a church planting team during these first two years, and attend classes twice a week for six months, similar to being a novice in the priesthood. After these two years there is a ceremony or ordination where each member prays over the new members, and everyone partakes of the Holy Communion together.

Beginning the third year, our members are able to become a team leader, and in the fourth year, they are allowed to be elected to the leadership council. We also encourage our members to consider making a commitment of permanence to our community. We follow these steps to encourage members to stop moving from one church or organization to another, just because of petty or flimsy reasons.

In addition to our disciplines, we encourage our missionaries to balance their work, ministry, family, and brokenness; and to live by faith and raise support. We raise support as a way of developing humility. We also engage in livelihood activities (part-time work) to augment our support. Married people are taught to make their marriage and families a higher priority than serving in the ministry. We welcome broken people to serve as wounded healers. We believe that we all came from a bad past until Christ saved us. We also believe we are all works in progress, which is precisely why we say we are on a journey. We have found Jesus but we also continue to look for Him. We have been saved fully and finally but we also continue to seek His salvation daily.

We make Christ real in our midst by competing to do the will of the Father. Jesus defined the boundaries of the church community when he said, my brother and my sister is he or she who does the will of the Father (Matthew 12:48-50). The boundary that divides our members from others is not just knowledge of the Bible, but obedience to the will of the

Father. The reality of Christ in our midst, or what we call The Body, is realized when there is an Olympiad inside the church, when all the members compete to do the will of the Father.

A few years ago, we conducted our silent retreat at the Gethsemane Prayer Mountain in Montablan. Another group was also there. One night, the other group prayed so loudly at the chapel on the cliff, the highest point of the retreat place. We were very annoyed because it was hard to concentrate praying with all the noise bouncing off the cliff. They shouted the same thing over and over again. *"Wala Kaming Alam!"* There is no exact English translation that captures the personal element of desperation, but it's something like "Oh God we are nothing, we know nothing, we are helpless without You!" As it went on, we began to feel shaken and bothered, unable to concentrate on praying. Their prayer had such a tremendous effect on us individually and it began to penetrate into our hearts. By afternoon we started to mimic them, half mockingly at first, but at night we shouted it at the top of our lungs. *Wala kaming alam!* This has been the most powerful prayer God has given us. It is the prayer of the poor, and one that we remember and treat as our motto.

2: The Living Gospel

Our vision is to build Christian communities in all the slums. We will not build or plant where there is already an existing church. The slums multiply at such a rapid pace that we will need to double or triple our efforts to even begin to catch up with urbanization.

Before we can evangelize, we need to first become a nation (as Israel was) and be a community (as the church is or is called to be). Abraham was called as one man but he was called to become a great nation so numerous that no one could count. In the Great Commission, witnessing was not a task given to individuals but the collective whole (plural) who live and follow God's laws together. What is on display is not our individual lives but how we interact as a community.

The most important reason Jesus left us was for the Holy Spirit to come. That way, Jesus is distributed to the entire Body. What Jesus could not do alone, the Body can do. He called his people to demonstrate community life together.

Jesus could not demonstrate forgiveness, sharing, love, and justice alone as one man. It could only be demonstrated by and within a community or family.

The Gospel is God's call to all the nations to watch and observe His people and see God's goodness. His people should be living examples of blessings and prosperity who share to the less fortunate. They don't ignore their poorer Christian brothers and sisters. Instead, they feed, clothe and take care of the poor and needy in their midst. When they have conflicts, they forgive and reconcile. The living Gospel is preached as an invitation for unbelievers to desire to become part of the community of God.

One major error in church doctrine is that justice and righteousness aren't practiced within the church, where it should initially be demonstrated. Social action should be practiced within the community before it is taught outside. Another error is the separation of rich and poor Christian communities. The rich Christians often worship in affluent suburbs and the poor in the slums. A poor believer may be converted through the social action of the rich, but when he arrives in their church he might realize a sense of exclusion. The justice and righteousness that converted him isn't being implemented inside the church. Beyond that, many rich Christians prefer attending services in churches where there are no poor members. Their excuses are mere arguments of inconvenience—unlike the rich, the poor (in the Philippines) will not understand sermons in English and they aren't garbed as fancily as the rich. This is a mockery of the Gospel. The Word of God must be more imperative and compelling, not easily set aside by such arguments.

The Bible says it isn't the poor who need to go to the rich church, but the other way around. It is the rich Christians who need to go to the poor church. The church needs the rich and the poor, the strong and the weak; otherwise it is not a church. It is not biblical to have an exclusively rich church or an exclusively poor church. We are cheating God if we say the Kingdom will only work if we have agreeable people inside the church, or only if we have our own kinds of people inside the church. It is precisely why our gospel is called the Gospel of reconciliation. Dietrich Bonhoeffer says we become a cult when we only want people like us in our church.

The real issue actually is this: Who is supposed to go where? Should the rich go to the poor church in Payatas (community near the garbage mountain) or the poor go to the rich church in Makati (financial district in Manila)? The answer is obvious. It is the rich who need the poor; thus, it is the rich who should go to the poor church. The poor do not need the rich so why should they bother going to Makati? Besides, it is the rich who have cars and can travel more easily. Why not follow the model of Jesus, to go to the poor, to be with the poor, to become poor?

Thomas Merton, a writer and mystic, affirmed this way of thinking. He asked the church to give up her desire for power and wealth. Merton advised the church to seek solidarity with the poor. The movement in the Bible is that of Christ's *kenosis*—this is a form of emptying oneself, just like Christ, to become poor in order to make others rich. The church is not called to become rich, but to become poor. It is a sin for the church to have a surplus. This call to destitution is for the church, not for individuals. But individuals who have this calling may also pursue voluntary destitution as an expression of their solidarity with the poor.

Many churches despise the poor. They would rather reach out to the wealthy and powerful. For them, planting churches in the slums is a dead-end thing because the poor cannot support the pastor, so the church would never become sustainable. What most churches do not realize is that if the church decides to focus on targeting the rich and powerful, the Gospel is automatically compromised. The church immediately loses its prophetic voice, and the right to speak against injustice and greed. Even before the first rich man is converted, the church is no longer able to speak against the status quo or even to want to change it because it is the status quo that supports and protects the rich and powerful. The church is trapped in a compromising position if it tries to get the favor of the rich and powerful.

The status quo is a system and a structure, operated by laws and norms, most of which are biased in favor of the top 1% of people in society. It is precisely these unjust laws that make them wealthy and powerful. The church can no longer speak out for higher minimum wages, and better working conditions, because these threaten the status quo. Calling for a change in the laws will antagonize the rich. This drives away the wealthy and powerful that the church has committed to reach out to; speaking out against the status quo would be counterproductive.

I was once with the Commissioner of Internal Revenue, on a mission to help the government to eliminate graft and corruption by promoting transparency. We were very positive because we had connections to many churches and thousands of church members. We promised the Commissioner that three months before the tax deadline every year, we would promote tax consciousness on the pulpit every Sunday and ask our congregations to pay their taxes in full. The Commissioner laughed and assured us that what we promised would never happen. He said, once we began speaking on the pulpit about tax compliance, our members would begin to leave the church. He was right. We were never successful. The churches could not make the pitch on the pulpit for fear of antagonizing the rich members, making them feel guilty that they were not paying their taxes correctly.

Christians cannot remain neutral. We are either for Jesus or against him. The whole world works on a dominant bias that is against the poor, and against Christ. Christians need to live counter-culturally, not just obeying Scripture but examining the underlying philosophical and ideological biases and working against them. Everyone is promoting an ideology and no one is neutral. We are either supporting the status quo or reforming it.

The church needs to see that the Kingdom works in an upside-down way which is the opposite of the law at work in the world. The lower we go the more Christ will lift us up. The lower we go in solidarity with the poor and oppressed, the more God will bring us to positions where we can speak to kings, billionaires and presidents. We saw this in the life of Mother Teresa, who constantly refused to become a celebrity but was also constantly thrust into the limelight.

Part of our self-critique, or what Paulo Freire calls conscientization, is to see in what way the church has become conformed to the world, or become worldly. The church needs to be counter-cultural, and is called to be salt and light, which means being a contrast society – in the world but not of the world. The church must live in such a way that the world is constantly being put on its toes. Self-critique can be done by looking at how the world is fast becoming secular and materialistic and how this has dehumanized people—fragmenting people (dividing heart from mind, soul and body) and isolating people (very individualistic and materialistic). In order to go against this trend, the church must seek to humanize people and the best way to do that is to bring people back again into community.

3: Holding all Things in Common

Wealth is measured more in how much we give than in how much we possess, accumulate, or hoard.

The Ondoy typhoon in 2009 was one of the worst to ever hit the Philippines. With unceasing rains coupled with strong winds, it left casualties in the thousands. People scattered the streets in the aftermath, whole communities were swept away, and billions of pesos worth of infrastructure was destroyed. Just a few hours after the sky's clearing, the people scanned their environment to assess the damage. There was a severe need for clean water, food and shelter. Our group distributed relief goods to more than 50,000 families. We understood how the goods needed to be delivered immediately, so as a policy the goods didn't stay with us for more than 24 hours. We would consider it a grave sin if they did.

One day we got a call from San Mateo; they had apparently not received any relief goods and had been without food for days. The water still hadn't subsided, and in some parts, it was still neck deep! Our supply of relief goods was already empty by the time we got the call; we had just given away our last batch.

The goods came from supporters; they gave either through cash or in kind. With our storage empty and with a desperate demand, we caught ourselves in a predicament. "Lord, what do we do now?" We prayed. It was 11:00am in the morning. I took a deep breath and slid out my credit card. It took me about two seconds to look at my card, before saying, "Call Suy Sing, and order goods for San Mateo!" (Suy Sing is the wholesale store that supplies goods to big grocery stores like Puregold, Hypermart, and Savemore.) Looking back, I remember the commingling of emotions. My stomach was already aching, but what was that, I wondered, compared to the hunger of the survivors? The need was urgent, but how was I ever going to pay for that one-thousand-dollar purchase?

Time was moving fast, and the ordering was taking a while. There was a lot of processing on the phone just to clear my credit card. We were about to finalize and confirm the payment, and then all of a sudden, a container van stopped in front of our office. It was a fresh supply of relief goods; enough for San Mateo! Relieved, I quickly took back my card. At that time, we had to act quickly to coordinate and deliver the goods—there was hardly any time to sit and reflect about the situation. But no matter how quickly we think we act, no one is faster than God. He is still faster than the swipe of a credit card or the issuing of checks. We are so afraid of losing what we have. We're afraid of becoming bankrupt. But what we don't know is that God is always faster than us. By the time we have given away one thousand dollars, God has given us ten thousand.

The church today needs to see that the call to become poor is not a call to desperation but a call to true faith. The tithes and offerings being collected in Sunday services are meant for the poor but the church often keeps it for its own comfort. We use the funds to pay for air-conditioning, carpets and luxurious buildings. We pay high salaries to our pastors and staff, to provide us the best, instead of blessing others. God does not consider this as giving at all. It is just giving to ourselves. After we have given our tithes (10%) in such churches, we still owe God our true tithes, which are meant for the poor. That means we have not really given yet.

The church that has given away everything can say to the beggar, *Silver and gold I have none but this I say unto you, arise in the name of Christ* (Acts 3:6). Giving our all is true wealth. But who will listen to that? Wealth in this world, even at times among Christians, is defined as hoarding, accumulating and amassing. It is keeping enough in a bank account to sustain a certain "lifestyle', to afford expensive things and important friends. The biblical definition of wealth is in contrast to the lifestyles that the rich have to uphold because of their social status. Wealth is about giving. It is about how much we give instead of how much we have kept or amass. It is about how much we have blessed others instead of how much we have kept for ourselves.

In the Bible, the value of a person's wealth is counted through their intense faith. That is what Jesus meant by the poor being rich in faith. He was adamant; radical in His teachings. *It is easier for a camel to enter the eye of a needle than for a rich man to enter the Kingdom* (Mark 10:25).

For many, material blessings are a sign of God's favor. We think God is looking at us through the clouds when we receive nice things. We feel at peace when we get what we want—peace with ourselves and with God. We humans are so gullible! If we find peace and happiness only in times of prosperity, what happens when we lose our prosperity all of a sudden? Do we also lose our peace? The book of Job asks an insane question: Should we receive only good things from God and not bad things?

As we mature, we realize that God's peace is found in His presence and nowhere else. Prosperity may be a sign of God's presence, and it is, but only a fragment. The bigger picture is that His grace is found primarily through suffering and need. For example, when someone donates a house and lot to us, we think that God loves us so much. There can't be any other explanation! But it may also be used by the devil, by influencing us to focus more on material pleasure than our spiritual walk. To realize God's peace is to be able to accept unfortunate things as from the Lord, just as we do the good things. The 13th century poet Rumi sums up this thought in a poem:

"...A joy, a depression, a meanness,
some momentary awareness comes
as an unexpected visitor.

Welcome and entertain them all!
Even if they're a crowd of sorrows...

Be grateful for whoever comes,
because each has been sent
as a guide from beyond."

Our profound fear of loss and poverty prevents us from giving biblically. If we see prosperity as the singular proof of God's presence, then we are living a life of fear. Once we've understood how to be grateful for every "visitor" as Rumi puts it, we've also understood God's true peace, one that does not stem from prosperity alone. This gives us the freedom to give—not for self-satisfaction, but willingly as to the Lord.

Giving in the Bible was illustrated as a lively and exciting contest. Beyond tithing, we are commanded to be cheerful givers. This is giving more than 10%. Cheerful givers give without counting every centavo (cent) like a part of them was taken away. They give with gratitude. It makes total sense that once we've taken to heart God's true peace in giving, we find the freedom to be cheerful about it! It is in man's nature to fear for shortage and lack. However, it is the Holy Spirit's work that penetrates through man's nature into his spirit that keeps him peaceful and cheerful.

The poor are the most cheerful givers. Many people think that the poor give an insignificant amount compared to the rich, but in fact it's the opposite. If I tell members of a rich church to religiously give 10% tithes, half of the church will try to bargain their way out. Some would even ask, gross or net? The poor, on the other hand, easily give more than 10%. If the poor give five hundred pesos (ten US dollars) in our church, we would look down on it even though it is already 100% of his or her surplus or disposable income. If a rich member gives one million pesos (twenty thousand US dollars), we quickly make him or her an elder even though that only represents less than 10% of his or her disposable income or surplus.

Many of our newer staff members at Companion With the Poor receive four-thousand pesos (about eighty US dollars) a month as support. One of our missionaries, after receiving his support, went straight to the supermarket to buy one-thousand pesos worth of groceries. Then he went straight to the hospital to visit a church member who had dengue fever. Along with the groceries, he also gave another one-thousand pesos to the member's family. In a matter of hours, he had already given away 50% of his monthly income! What's more, he kept looking that day for more ways he could give.

Being cheerful however does not mean we are now in the competition. The Apostle Paul recorded the sacrificial giving of the poor Macedonians, who gave beyond their means, showing that it is sacrificial giving that entitles us to join the contest—which is God's exciting challenge for us. We must sense this in God's Word when He said, put me to the test, "Give!" (Malachi 3:10) In another part, He also said, *As you have given, I will also give back to you. What I give back will be pressed tightly, shaken until it is really dense, and made to overflow* (Luke 6:38). This is a picture of abundant generosity. It is a contest.

The final bout comes after the contest. We must be angry; even more than angry. We must be so angry and mad that we want to get even. I learned this from a dear friend, Anthony. After his son was successfully operated on, he went to the stage and thanked the church, for all he had received. But he ended it by saying that he would get even. He was mad because now he had been outdone. He knew that it is more blessed to give than to receive and he had just received so much. He knew then that those who had given more would get more blessings! He did not want to lose in this game of one-upmanship, so he needed to give more than those who gave to him.

Filipinos would have less disdain for the poor if we realized that in the last few decades, it has been the poor who saved the Philippines from bankruptcy. Overseas Filipino Workers (OFWs), most taking blue-collar jobs as domestic helpers, seamen, construction workers, factory workers and nurses, migrate to strange lands with an entirely different language and culture to earn money to send back home. Despite stories of abuse and displacement, they continue to live simply so they can give their income back to their families in the Philippines. The OFWs contribute more than twenty billion US dollars annually to our economy and it is increasing every quarter. Not even the top ten Philippine companies combined contribute that much. But why do we hate the poor so much? Why do we look down on them so much?

This brings us back to my narrative at the beginning of this chapter. During the relief operations for the super-typhoon Ondoy, dozens of our poor pastors and friends flocked to our office. They were pressing us to somehow get them involved. They had no money to donate but I felt that their hearts were bursting to give, to do anything to help. Every day they arrived at four in the morning and worked until midnight. They helped lifting heavy sacks of rice and boxes of clothing, packing groceries, and sorting all the donations. Their labor to the poor and the flood victims was their way of giving back to God.

Wealth is measured more in how much we give than in how much we possess or accumulate. It is not a matter of amount but of selflessness. The poor give more than the rich when counted in percentage. Beyond financial giving, the poor also give all of themselves to those who need more than they do. Thus, the rich must catch up with the poor to out-give them.

Reflections on *Community* from CWTP Missionaries

Community is full of pains, joys, and many other things. It's like a cake—the ingredients themselves are not enjoyed alone, but when put together, it's great. – Bart

CWTP taught me to depend on others, especially because

I'm stubborn and independent...when it's my turn to ask for help, I tend to be withdrawn. I'm used to always helping others, but now I'm learning to accept other people's kindness as well. – Talah

We have a profound sense of community. We are a caring and supporting body or community. We love, care for, and cherish each other deeply. – Joji

The truth is I haven't been here for long yet, but so far this is what I've noticed: No one is higher or lower than another, but what matters is how you humble yourself and how you relate with the poor. – Oseth

The community of CWTP is well organized and fun. Because of this community, I feel more human. – Asher

"As a community composed of different personalities, perspectives, and beliefs, we look like a real family, real human beings – in the world but not of the world. We share, we laugh and cry together, we fight, and we still manage to hug and hold each other genuinely." – Chein

My love for the Lord has deepened and so has my desire to serve Him. There are so many hardships in the community, but the more you embrace your love for the Lord, despite these hardships, the more you glorify Him. There is equal love here...even though some of us are attorneys, and others have several degrees, we are all equal. No one is higher or lower than the other, and those who are 'higher' are very humble. There is love and care. – Paulette

I found another family in Companion. I started in 2006, just hoping, no plan, no idea about CWTP (it was MMP before), and not even a hint that I'd become part of the leadership. I started growing and finally became in love with the community because I experienced the love, care and acceptance. I have seen how the members of the community love each other, and how they serve one another by sharing their resources. I experienced that I was important and became accepted. – Ely

*I am thankful to the Lord that I became part of the CWTP family. I have grown spiritually and emotionally. I have also learned that I can say what I want, and not just what I need. I've learned to be confident here.
– Flor*

I experienced here the real meaning of unity, cooperation and a helping hand; most of all, having one heart to love one another – a real family. I also learned to be even better in sharing the Word of God. – Delia

Three things I enjoyed in CWTP: Connection- connecting with other people, including foreigners. Correction- a lot of things have been corrected with me, and my views in life. Collection- I've collected good memories, ideas, strategies, and God's message. – Ramon

In our work together as companions with the  *poor, we learn that each has something to give no matter how small. We learn and still continue to learn to listen to each other's stories and through it make ways of connection from being closed to being open, from being alone to being together, journeying toward the heart of God. – Leo*

 *I am grateful to our Lord Jesus Christ that I am part of CWTP. It has a unity and concern for one another, especially if there's a problem; the community becomes concerned and gives their time and advice without judgment. I enjoy being here and CWTP is my family. It is not just a community but also a family.*
– Maria

Because of CWTP, I better understnd the meaning of community life. Through our community, I have learned how to offer my heart. – Winston

The community life is solid. We learn to help one another, be full of grace, and identify those in need. We also help each other through counseling and spiritual direction. There is a real balance and sense of family. – Jannette

I am glad that I have brothers and sisters in the Lord, treating one another as a family, in the community of CWTP. I have felt and experienced how the community gives importance to one another and the love that comes from the Lord. – Julie

My experiences in CWTP are wonderful. They have helped me greatly to develop my personality. – Jeff

CWTP for me is a family, a companion and help in times of need. A family that does the purpose of Christ, bringing the Kingdom of God on earth as it is in heaven. We get to journey as companions with one another no matter

what we are going through and help each other in times of need. – Raymond

Part 2:
The Poor

4: Journeying with the Poor

We are called to journey with the poor in downward mobility.

I think the best way to remove our blinders or prejudices against the poor is to really get to know them. In the last 40 years of working among the poor, I can still count with one hand the number of rich people who really know the poor. Many have their biases, some even with extreme misconceptions of the poor. They think the poor are lazy, resigned in their misery without trying to alleviate their situation. Many of the rich are not aware of their privilege; thinking that solely having dreams and hard work are enough to lift someone out of poverty. Of course, the rich also become successful because of good education and hard work, but the poor aren't as fortunate. They cannot afford progressive schools, and they have a much harder time making ends meet.

Because of the wide division among the rich and the poor, their communities are also different. Their neighborhoods, schools, churches, markets and means of transportation are separate. Because of this, their friends, their children's friends and the strangers they bump into belong to the same social class. This makes it difficult for the rich to have a fair and true account of how the poor really experience reality. Their only peek into the reality of the poor in the Philippines is through media—news about mothers with ten children needing health care, or the growing drug epidemic, poverty-driven crime and other issues totally unrelated to them. They think the poor will just take advantage of their kindness. Many believe that it's a waste of time to minister to the poor. They think it is the poor who need them and that they are the ones doing the poor a favor.

I've never had difficulty adjusting in the slums. Maybe because my teenage years were spent among them. We weren't exactly poor but my parents were always away and the only friends I could find were our poor neighbors. It was a kid's natural way of breaking the walls of prejudice. I felt very comfortable with them and considered them my best friends.

Of course, the poor in the slums are different from the poor that sleep on the streets and under bridges. In developed countries or even among the rich in the Philippines, a beggar in ragged clothes is the common image when we hear the word "poor". These poor individuals are treated as the dregs of society, especially since they cannot keep up with the rapid pace of life in a modernizing society. Most of them are alcoholics, parolees, or drug addicts; and most suffer from depression, sexual exploitation, or even PTSD. They are rich in stories and life experiences, but cannot keep a job or a family. Most of them can be found in food queues in big cities, or begging on the street corners. Most of the time, you will need a PhD in psychology to be able to minister to them.

The poor living in the slums in the Philippines on the other hand, and even the refugees and immigrants in developed countries, are different. For them, it is often their lack of access to health care, good schools, jobs, and financial institutions that prevent them from moving out of poverty. When the poor are connected to these networks and opportunities, like in our work in the slums in the Philippines, they often turn around and move out of poverty quite quickly.

We must understand the poor to be able to journey with them. Most of the people in Companion With the Poor come from and still live in the slums. We have other members who decide to live in the slums even though they weren't originally from there. Either way, all of our missionaries are required to do immersion trips into the slums, or visit other slums different from their own, from a few days up to a few years.

When we journey with the poor, it is to find out how they live. We remove our gaze from a higher social or economic class. We try to relate to them and understand their spirituality. When we do immersion, we experience the miserable conditions that are considered normal by more than a third of the world's population. Those who 'immerse' choose to live among the poor with the intention of learning how to journey with the poor. We seek to enter into their lives and find out how they understand and express their faith and spirituality. It is far more important to learn to journey with the poor than to promote so-called development work. We must first understand why God said the poor are rich in faith. What is important is being able to see Jesus in the poor, the dying, and in the sick. Helping the poor rise out of poverty is only secondary.

Immersion is not just being there physically. Many missionaries put in a lot of effort based on their drivenness to help the poor rather than from Christ in their hearts. If you put them in solitary confinement for even a few days, they would go crazy. Immersion can only be done through solitude. This ability to be present to God in all our moments is how we can really journey with the poor and then begin to see Jesus in them. It takes a lot of practice of being present to the Lord and present to those around us to be able to do that.

Once in the slums, our sense of well-being will be challenged. When my students go to the slums, I instruct them not to bring more money than needed. They should carry the same amount as the average person living in the slums. One time, a student called me to ask how much he should allocate for his food during immersion. I never thought of it and just blurted out, 10 pesos (20 US cents) per meal! My wife overheard the conversation, giving me a petrified look for that risky estimate.

It is often difficult to adjust to the new environment while in immersion. Once, during the first night of the immersion, one of my students panicked and ran to the church at three in the morning when he heard the couple next door having sex. He was so shocked; after all, only a cardboard wall separated him from them. There is no privacy in the slums, neither are there amenities—toilets, running water, or electricity. Epidemics and malnutrition are frequent and rampant. Rats and maggots creep into every nook and cranny of sleeping areas, or crawl over your body when you sleep at night.

Some enter the slums with a paternalistic attitude, to give to the poor. They think the poor cannot teach us anything about spirituality, and that they are all dysfunctional and needy. This image is very hurtful to the poor. Some bring food and money to the slums, throwing feasts and lavish generous gifts on their hosts. This is the reverse of journeying with the poor; it is in fact, journeying with the rich. We ask the poor to journey with us, not the opposite. If the poor come and see how we live and how luxurious our lives are, they will compare themselves and begin to feel small. To journey, we need to let go of our resources and live where they live, eat what they eat. I tell our hosts in the slums to avoid buying or preparing anything special for us. It will not help us understand the situation and lifestyle of the poor.

When we learn to journey with the poor, we will also begin to see and learn from their faith. Not only do we get to experience how they live, but we also begin to see the stories and lives of ordinary people. There are lots of stories of members of Companion With the Poor who have chosen to journey with the poor on a daily basis. Astrid, one of our retired missionaries, was always seen giving a lot of her financial support to the poor that she encountered on the way home, even though she, too, had very little to live on. Imee, as a matter of habit, would bring home the remaining bowls of soup from our gatherings to distribute to her neighbors in Payatas. Many in CWTP borrow money just to be able to attend our worship every other Wednesday. The CWTP offering plate is not for our organization. It is collected for those who attend who had to borrow money just to get to our place of worship and have no money to get home. They can also take an additional amount for their lunch, so they don't have to suffer the indignity of asking for money.

Because most of us are very poor, a prayer common to us is for the provision of food. One of our partner pastors was once on special ops in the mountains of Davao, evangelizing to the T'boli tribes. He would wait at the Philippine Air Force base for a seat in one of the giant C130's, a remnant from WWII. It's very interesting because he is so poor but he can casually leave our office in Quezon City and the next moment, be in General Santos 16,000 kilometers away. The flight is free because it is a government plane, but he will stand the entire trip. Within the same day he will call to say he is already in General Santos, beginning his trip to the mountains.

Back at the office he would tell us stories about his mission. They are usually stories of survival without money or food. During one hike up a hill, he was very hungry and he had no food with him. He had to rely on God and good Samaritans to feed him. On time, he even prayed that he could just eat the leaves or plants along the trail and God would make his stomach able to digest them—and God answered his prayer!

We are like the monks who live in the slums, and not in the monastery. Many monks hide away in the monastery but we hide away in the poorest sector of the city. The slum is not a place as much as a way of life, a journey to obscurity—to become unknown and forgotten—forgotten by the world, by our friends and by our families. Once the monk enters the monastery, he also becomes unknown, forgotten, by all but God. It is a way of life we have embedded in our hearts through silent retreats and solitude, so wherever we are, whatever we are doing, we are on that journey to obscurity.

Monks do their work in secret through the divine offices. In doing this, they do the work of God through prayer as God works through them and in the world through their prayers.

As the Psalmist says, *Seven times a day I praise You for Your righteous laws.* And also, *In the middle of night I rise to give thanks for Your righteous laws* (Psalm 119:164). It is always a prayer at work, what the Jesuits call contemplation in action. We seek to make Christ real through the practice of the presence of God taught by Brother Lawrence, so that at all times, we are able to see God's presence in the poor, the dying, and the sick, and they are able to see God's presence in us. Our work is to call forth God's beauty and peace in and through the chaos and oppression of the slums, not in order to become experts or celebrities, but through a true walk into oblivion, to become one with the poor.

5: Reading the Bible from the Bottom Up

*We need to learn to read the Bible from the bottom-up,
from the perspective of weakness and poverty and not
from the perspective of power and wealth.*

Our interpretation of the Bible has been hijacked by the rich.
We've been trained to believe that success as Christians
means being financially superior and having church services
in opulent cathedrals. Rich Christians often read the Bible
from the perspective of power and wealth. Because of this,
poor Christians tend to read the Bible in the same way, and
thus view themselves as powerless and weak.

It is important to read the Bible from the perspective of
poverty and weakness. About 90% of Christians around the
world are poor. Reading the Bible from the bottom-up
results in a Gospel that will produce hermeneutics that
benefit the poor, instead of sanctifying their oppression.
Theology has always been written from the 10% that owns
90% of the world's wealth. For that matter, their theology

will never question the serious inequality of the status quo that has marginalized 90% of the world. Learning to read the Bible from the bottom-up will result in theology being drawn from below, from the perspective of the majority. It is uncanny that the Bible, which is a book for the poor, should be controlled and interpreted by the dominant few and sometimes used to oppress the majority who are poor.

Brian Zahnd, a wealthy Egyptian Christian living in Greece pointed out the incongruity of the Bible. I think he has put his finger correctly on what it means to read the Bible from the bottom-up when he said that history is always written from the perspective of the victors (Greece, Rome, Egypt, Babylon, Assyria, etc.). But the Bible is actually written from the perspective of the losers, the marginalized and the oppressed. We have sought to write this book following that thought, to provide ammunition to subvert the status quo by writing so that the oppressed, weak and poor may know how to critique the theology of the rich and powerful.

The easiest way to learn to read from the bottom-up is to see life from the perspective of the majority. Some rich people think that I am being ideological when I say this, but really, no one is free from ideology. We either have an ideology that favors the rich or an ideology that favors the poor. We always read the Bible with an ideological bias.

Since no one is neutral and all theology is biased, we must intentionally seek to be biased for the poor or for the majority. This is also true when it comes to the general way of life, in the way that the society is dehumanizing people. We must be intentionally counter-cultural in order to balance, if not go against, the outright secularization being promoted by present day Christianity. The Bible is clearly biased for the majority and is clearly upside down (from the bottom to the top). The Bible promotes an upside-down perspective, saying that *the first shall be last, the weak shall be made strong,* and *the person who loses his life will gain it* (Matthew 19:20; 1 Corinthians 1:27-28). Jesus promoted this perspective by emptying himself (kenosis) and becoming a human being. He commanded that all his disciples become servants of all.

Many Western missionaries could never understand this. The royalties of England debated and killed each other on the issue of the divine rights of kings; but they could not see that while God indeed makes one a king, he does so not so that he can have his way or push people around. God wants us to rule by becoming servants. Many Western missionaries tell me that there is no more role for them in the Philippines. But if they realize their misunderstanding of the role of a servant, they would come back and repair the mess they have created.

For years, we saw the Western missionaries do ministry and then turn them over to the Filipinos. They viewed that act as the noblest act of all. But they could not see that it was really their independence and their refusal to work together with the locals that was being promoted. After they had turned over the work, they would leave us. But what was then, and is still now needed, is for them to come and model for us the true missionary spirit, which is to come and work under the leadership of the locals. There are many who do incarnational ministry who cannot even imagine working under the locals. They actually maintain their tight circle of rich Western missionaries, holding the locals at arms-length so they cannot enter or join. They are physically together in the slum only. The right to vote, the decision on finances, and even leadership itself are all beyond the powers of the locals.

Everything in the world today is biased against the poor and the odds are all stacked against the majority of the people of the world. We must thus be good students of the status quo and learn to critique it; and to see the ideological and philosophical biases of the modern Gospel.

We are reminded of the story of the widow's mite, where the widow gives her only two coins while wealthy people gave so much more. Jesus told His disciples that what she offered is much more valuable than those of the rich, because she gave everything she had. The story of the widow's mite tells us the difference between giving more and giving sacrificially. We learn from the story that God indeed sees the sacrificial giving of the poor. This can be an example of reading the Bible from the bottom-up.

Good theology considers the critical fact that the status quo is oppressive because 10% of the people own 90% of the world's wealth. The Bible always focuses on the poor. While it also talks about the figurative poor, the Bible talks so much about the penniless, widows and orphans who are lowest in societal position. The Bible looks up at and lifts up the poor, just as in the widow's mite story. Jesus lifted up and praised the poor widow, which in many rich Western hermeneutics is completely ignored. In present reality, the sacrifices and gifts of the poor are ignored or downgraded, to give focus on the actions and gifts of the rich, which are higher in number and amount. Yet in the widow's mite, God's gaze is on the value and sacrifice of the poor.

The great reversal is another case in point. The Bible is punctuated by these alarm signals of a day when things will be turned upside down – those who laugh now will cry, those who are filled now will be hungry, those who are powerful now will be cast down, and those who are living in affluence now, like in the story of Lazarus, will become pitiful. The Magnificat actually throws the challenge this way: whose side will you be on in that fateful day of reversal? The Magnificat says the hungry will be filled with good things and the rich sent away empty! It is a scary thing to be found on the wrong side and yet we have minimized this so much in our reading of Scripture because we read it from the perspective of those who will be upturned and cast out or cast down. We do not want to read about our own indictment.

We do not want to hear denunciation of the rich and powerful in the Bible. Even the poor among us don't want to read it this way because we all want to become wealthy—a result of the materialistic bias of Christianity. We read the Bible from top to bottom when we ignore Jesus' curse on the rich. The statement "the poor are rich in faith" in James is falsely referred to the symbolic poor, not the literal or economic poor, which is the obvious sense in the context. By saying the poor can mean both rich and poor, we have rendered the text inutile and meaningless. James is very outspoken against the rich. To read the Bible with that spirit in mind, is to begin to read the Bible from the bottom-up.

The spirit of the rich who have hijacked the Bible is characterized by an anti-poor attitude, looking down on the poor and rejecting the downward mobility of Jesus—who though he was rich became poor in order to make others rich. No one can be neutral on this. Either we look down on the poor as many rich Christians do now or look down on the rich as the Bible actually does. The Bible promotes this downward mobility, to become poor in order to make others rich.

6: Cultivating Fortitude

Therefore, let us leave the elementary doctrine of Christ and go on to maturity, not laying again a foundation of repentance from dead works and of faith toward God.
– Hebrews 6:1

Before my personal encounter with Jesus, I used to smoke two packs of cigarettes a day. Those who've had this habit understand how difficult it is to quit smoking, especially with such a heavy daily dose. I tried several times to quit, or even to lessen my intake but to no long-term avail. After I experienced Jesus for the first time, it's like my smoking addiction was hit by a truck and was knocked out of my body. Bam! I was able to quit!

There is hardly a more apt term to describe my encounter with Jesus than as *real*. It was the real thing! I knew this within myself because I saw my life turn around with little effort on my part. Quitting smoking seemed such an easy task; it seemed such a small change brought by the new energy I felt. Suddenly I had purpose, a new outlook and lifestyle that stemmed from my first encounter with Jesus.

The Bible, which to me used to be just a series of texts not unlike other inspirational books, suddenly had meaning. It became alive, speaking to me on a personal level and inflaming a light inside me.

A week or two after that encounter, I saw a man light a cigarette in a store and I felt really angry. I thought, "How could that man not realize the sacredness of the human body, that it is the embodiment of something as precious as God himself? Why is he destroying his body?" I caught myself in that moment of anger and realized I hadn't smoked a single cigarette since I encountered Jesus. For the first time, I understood what it meant to be spiritually cleansed—not just free of the weight of my sins but also free from its power. Before I was born-again, I was enslaved by sin. It imprisoned me in a way that I didn't have a choice but to do wrong. Now I was given the choice to follow Christ or Satan. I talked to Christ every day and sought his will in everything in order to conform myself to his purpose. The reality of Christ was firmly set in my life. This is important because the reality of Christ is what is supposed to keep us going in our Christian life.

Many Christians seek to understand Christ through the intellect alone. Although studying the Bible is integral to Christianity, it is the pursuit of the experiential Christ that leads to a contemplative life. Experiencing the reality of Christ is an excitement that fuels our inner being—not in the way of cheap thrills like roller coasters or caffeine highs but something that truly changes a person's interior and outlook. We are addicted to excitement, whether through the adrenaline rush of frenzied experiences or new things. The rush that we feel upon encountering Christ does not stem from our need for excitement and restlessness, but from a deep longing that can never be filled through worldly means. Experiencing Christ affects every aspect of our lives the way sunshine penetrates through every dark crevice. It is positive energy in its purest sense—light, warm, and exciting to share with others.

As we grow in our faith, the excitement from the first born-again experience fades. The passionate dialogues grow into silent soliloquies. Many born-again people, after thirty or forty years, feel that God is no longer there. God is silent. God is distant. Many leave their evangelical churches not because they have lost their faith, but because they no longer experience the epiphany and fervent emotion that they long for. With or without the experience of spiritual thrill, spirituality is a journey. It is the constant search and emotional connection with Jesus. It is not a one-time ecstasy that one has to recreate in order to keep the faith. It is a journey, one that resembles our relationship with other people. If we have a miserable relationship with the people around us, our "terrific" relationship with Jesus should be suspect, or put in doubt.

As we grow old, we realize God doesn't answer all our prayers, not because He doesn't hear them but because we are focused on our comforts instead of on our willingness to suffer for Jesus. We understand that God works in mysterious ways. He is hidden, only appearing when sought for. C.S. Lewis describes his presence and absence as falling behind into the shadows. We must change our perspective of reality. We should always view things from the reality of God, which is greater and stronger than our limited view in our own lives.

When the thrill of our spiritual mountains is absent, we need to cultivate fortitude. Fortitude is staying steadfast and courageous despite pain. This is something we develop through years of obedience and humility—our experiences of highs and lows make our faith resilient. Whatever happens, we must be faithful. This is an inner strength that will not succumb to sin despite our doubts about God. Ceaseless prayer is also important. Despite our doubts, spiritual deserts, and moments when we think God is absent, our honest and raw prayers must persevere.

It is important to find Jesus in our everyday lives, no matter how unspectacular they may seem. This is the ancient practice of *Examen* of consciousness. Before going to bed, we should ask, "Where was God in my life today?" This daily spiritual discipline gradually etches and places Christ's image in us. It is a practice that alerts us to the possibility of epiphany—being vigilant and alert to his presence. The *Examen* sharpens our discernment.

As I developed as a person, I began to sense and understand God's reality. It's different from when I first encountered Him, which was a powerful rush in my system. Through the years, He stayed with me through pleasant blessings and painful situations. As I grew both physically and spiritually, I was able to discern God both in joy and pain, teaching me to be brave in accepting not just happy and light experiences, but also heavy and confusing ones. For example, I used to always distract myself from loneliness. It's an awful feeling that ruins relationships and productivity. When I learned to journey with God in the everyday, running away from loneliness seemed so ridiculous. I was able to completely embrace my loneliness and channel it to Jesus. My loneliness stemmed from a deep longing for Him that I could never fill with being busy or being distracted by material things.

I found freedom in Christ, which at the beginning seemed such an abstract concept. My interaction with Jesus has become more relaxed, playful and gracious. My relationship with God used to be prone to stress, guilt and pressure, but now I experience a calm—probably similar to the Psalmist's laying down in green pastures and walking beside still waters. Although the very presence of Jesus is fleeting, I find Him in many of my relationships and experiences. It is a grateful acceptance of small joys—even in the everyday hustle with my three loving sons and wife. Their faith in me keeps me in line and keeps me from becoming an insensitive jerk. I guess the biggest difference is that Jesus is more engaged with me; or rather more of me is available to Him. It is the freedom that one receives after complete surrender and trust. It is a love shared beyond the intellect—He wants me to love him with all my heart, soul and body.

Today, there is a big change in the way I look at the Bible. The Bible is no longer just a manual for correct living or a code of ethics, as much as a pair of lenses to help me see reality. If I were to imagine what would happen if God were suddenly present with me to dwell among men, things would drastically change. Things I thought were important would begin to move to the back and certain things would be highlighted—truth, righteousness, love, compassion, forgiveness—these are what is real when God is in our midst.

7: Companions with the Poor

We are a community on a spiritual journey. Our community is for the poor.
Thus, our name: Companion With the Poor.

I've been working in the slums for four decades now. Every day is a lesson of perseverance and purposefulness, but at times I couldn't help feeling burnt out. One time, I was standing over the garbage mountain in Payatas. An average of 2,000 garbage trucks would dump their load there daily, attracting a community of 3,000 scavengers. I was facing the dumpsite with the dust flying towards me, forcing the smell of the garbage into my throat. I was depressed. I grounded myself too much in that moment—my skin could only feel the thick layer of dust mixed with my sweat; and I could only hear the noisy children running around, the trucks zooming by, and the flies buzzing in and out of my ear. I thought about my friends from law school. We were from the best university in the country, and while they were enjoying luxurious suites, I was standing in the garbage dump without enough money to send my kids to school. I pitied myself.

It was a young scavenger who led me back to reality. He was one of thousands who collected recyclables from the garbage mountain. He walked up to me and engaged me in a conversation. He said that one time, he and his fellow scavengers spent the night in an empty container van. One night, one of his fellow scavengers was high on *shabu* (local methamphetamine). While everyone was asleep, his friend woke up raving mad and stabbed all of the men in the van. The man I was talking to was the only survivor. He was brought to the hospital and left with a big question about the meaning of life. He went from one religious community to another – from groups in Mt. Banahaw to Mt. Samat – but found no answer. One day he was in his shack (I remembered that I had been there before; it had just the earth as floor), and he saw two men passing by. He called out to them, "Who are you and what are you doing?" They said they were evangelists and were sharing about salvation in Jesus. So he said, "Come, share it with me." Afterwards, he knelt before the two men and prayed to receive Jesus.

I was so shocked! If there was a single moment in my life where I was so sure God was talking to me, it was that time. I asked the young man what his name was, and he said, "My name is Nicodemus." I almost cried. My depression lifted immediately; even the scenery didn't seem as harsh. Before, I was blinded by the dust and smell of the garbage; but now, I could see Jesus walking through the garbage, looking for Nicodemus. From there I recalled Jesus saying, "Where I am, there my servants will be" (John 12:26). I knew then that mission meant to be where Jesus was. And if Jesus were in the dumpsite, I would go there to be with him.

A few years later, I met a man named Lando while planting a church in Bansalangin, Payatas. This was years before we were part of CWTP. We fought for land rights and socialized housing projects in the barangay, where more than five-hundred families were made beneficiaries.

Lando studied Agriculture in the best state university in the Visayas region. He came from a family of fishermen. He had to provide for the rest of his siblings, so he migrated to Manila to find better pastures. Without much guidance, he became manager of a three-hundred sow farm beside our church, which was not really a farm in a decent sense. It was almost like running a farm in the middle of the city market. All the pigs were fed food scraps culled from the garbage dumpsite. It seemed like a second level dumpsite itself. The food scraps were always alive and moving—with maggots. He became a Christian through the Lakas Angkan campus ministry. When we started our church, he joined and immediately became one of the leaders. He was a natural-born teacher and those who attended his Bible studies grew and matured in their faith.

He later married Josie, who worked as a domestic worker in Hong Kong. They were classmates in the state university back home. She had a degree in Agriculture Economics. She gave up a good income to marry Lando and live in Bansalangin. Eventually, they were pushed to extreme poverty and landed beside the garbage mountain. When I saw him again, he was in a shack, with the ground as his floor. They had one room and a run-down sewing machine where they made rugs from scraps from the garbage mountain. They were living in extreme poverty but still in love with Jesus. Plus, they now had a baby, Rapha Joy.

Upon my invitation, Lando joined Mission Ministries Philippines (this was before we became CWTP) and soon rose from the ranks to become a team leader. His income and support base improved and he was soon out of the garbage dumpsite, into a more decent house. MMP lent him money for raising pigs, goats and a tricycle (Kawasaki motorcycle with a side car). His Bible studies were quite extraordinary. In MMP, he would always have the most number of Bible study groups, more than one a day! Lando planted many churches and we saw a big future for him, maybe even someday becoming our Executive Director. Eventually, they had another child, Gwyneth. Josie then landed a permanent job at the church as a preschool teacher. MMP sent her to get a Masters in preschool management. All the time, they lived like ordinary slum families do.

Lando suffered serious asthma, as I do. I was the only one who could afford the expensive sprays—Nasonex, Symbicort, and others. The rest took hand-me-downs from me. We shared our spray medicines. Sometimes I would buy two and would give it to each one of them, by turns.

Around midnight in 2009, we received a distress call. Lando had an asthma attack and was having trouble breathing. They did not know what to do. My wife, who is a doctor, told them to rush him to the hospital but judging by her facial expression, I knew it was over. We got dressed and got to the hospital where his body lay. We lost a really good worker. Lando still remains with us in spirit, always a reminder of sacrifice and perseverance. He will always be a model for us of what a good Bible study teacher is.

Over time, we have also had a few non-Filipinos join our ministry. In the past few years, there have been three Americans living and working with us in the slums, and a few others from Korea, Australia, Singapore, Japan, Canada, and the UK helping us too. The founders of MMP are also American citizens, although one is a Filipino by birth. When the foreigners came, it really took us by surprise. We were wondering what God was up to. After praying and discerning, we realized it may be that God is telling us that our journey does not belong to Filipinos alone, but also to the rest of the world. Our ministry suddenly has gotten very small—located on a few tiny islands and dots on the ocean. We are encouraged to look to a wider horizon of God's work all around the world.

Reflections on *The Poor* from CWTP Missionaries

Our ministry isn't easy but there is a joy in serving the Lord. Though sometimes I get tired, deep inside my heart I am happily serving the Lord. – Rebecca

It's been great because I understand the community life of the poor, and I learn a lot from them. I always learn something new every day. – Michael

Knowing that God is already ahead of us in an urban poor area where we are going to plant a church is like finding a treasure. The church we planted in Villa Alfonso, Las Pinas, Metro Manila, transformed ordinary men into leaders. There were nine of them and their means of livelihood were scavenging, fruit and vegetable vendors, taxi drivers, rubber pot making and fishermen. They were living beside a garbage dumpsite, but you could feel that they are the happy poor because of the longing for God in their lives. – Marcelo

I really enjoy being part of this community. More than just an organization that plants churches, starts preschools, and does development work, it is a community journeying with Jesus. Helping with  *food, housing, water, and education are all good things, but that doesn't make us a Christian community. The thing that defines us is the fact that we really desire to know Jesus more, and when people see us, they see Jesus.*
– Paul

 *I learned to embrace the contradictions of life and relationships. I also learned to be gracious to others and accept grace from others.*
– Mila

Our ministry is challenging but also very gratifying. It is gratifying because we have our spiritual family, where we can truly feel love, moral support, and financial support. Through that, we have the  *perseverance to continue God's work even though it's tough at times. It's challenging in a sense that among the urban poor, the community experiences so many hardships. You'll see a lot of tensions stemming from poverty, but it's a real privilege to serve the Lord because He loves the poor so much. – McLloyd*

I learned a lot, and I can say that I've seen the movement of the Lord in our activities. – Marvin

There are a lot of challenges in our ministry areas. You cannot help getting deeply affected by the stories of the families in these communities. In CWTP, we have a very good  *companionship. We have a high regard for each other, and also care deeply for each other. You can feel this with the leaders too. I like how they carry out their leadership; they also have a high regard for the missionaries under their authority. – Ronnel*

 *Urban poor ministry is no easy task. I sacrifice a lot of things, but it is in order to understand the real meaning of God's love. – Eric*

My experience in CWTP is colorful. Colorful because there is always a mixture of emotions and experiences, like tears and joy, hardships and easiness. And in all of it the Lord is our constant  *companion in every experience. – Liway*

For me, all that I've experienced and will experience are challenges. Going to the area is challenging but also fulfilling. We go even when the weather is bad, when it rains hard and the ground is slippery, or when it's very hot. There are also times when I get sick, get dizzy and have headaches. It's very difficult but fulfilling, especially when you become part of the community. You grow to love the people there, and you can really be part of the 'Great Commission'. – Ligaya

I enjoy the community life, going to the areas, and interacting with people from all walks of life. I love playing with the kids too, but the most pleasant of all is witnessing all the lives that God changed in every community. After two years, it's good to look back and see how God moves in every area that we work in. – Queenie

 *As someone who has seen CWTP from its birth pains to where it is now, it has come a long way. It began from six couples and a single lady. Now, it has grown to more than 50 missionaries.* God continues to amuse and amaze us of His handiwork and continues to inspire us of the work among the poor and through the people whom God has called and uses for His kingdom. – Don

 *I learned to interact with strangers. I grasped how important my obligation is to my community, and I learned humility* and how to ask forgiveness when I make mistakes. I saw what it means to be a true Son of God — to be there for one another and to love the Lord with all our heart, mind, and soul. Being a missionary is difficult, but also fulfilling, just like the life of Christ. – Joel

"Not only in word, but in deed." This is how CWTP functions. In loving the poor, I learned to embrace the life of poverty and to work in poor communities. I also learned how to be silent, not only in sound (I am very talkative), but also in silencing my heart in our prayers and silent retreats. – Margery

CWTP's ministry among the poor is thriving; and it is filled with joy and excitement. There is joy in serving and reaching out to the underserved and unreached. And there is joy in learning to embrace and wash each other's feet..."do as I have done to you" (John 13:14-15). – Joyce

Part 3: Solitude

8: Finding our Solitude

Our hope is that through the discipline of Solitude, what Brother Lawrence called "The Practice of the Presence of God," we may be instilled with a spiritual strength that is able to see Jesus in the sick, the dying and the poor, like Mother Teresa always taught.

In 2000, I enrolled in a graduate diploma program in Spiritual Direction. It wasn't until completing this course that I began to see more clearly the interior part of my spiritual life. From my observation, and experience before enrolling in this program, very few evangelicals have an interior spirituality. Yet, like an insect being drawn toward a lightbulb, the more I began to pray during this time, the more I was drawn into the contemplative arena.

Before enrolling, a deep sense of burn-out pervaded my life. I longed for rest, to disappear, or just to hide from everyone and everything. I longed to bring my family to Minneapolis, where my sister lived. I asked God, "Just give me one year off!"

As usual, God had a different plan. My wife and I, along with five others from Manila, landed in Tao Fung Shan, Hong Kong, and enrolled in the two-year program in Spiritual Direction. Instead of being given refuge in a basement in Minneapolis, my wife and I (along with the others) were given a special guided retreat in a monastery for two years.

It was here that I began to experience silence, solitude, and the music of Taize; music and spirituality that has become such a part of who we are as a community today. At the time though, and even after graduating from the program, those of us who attended this training really rebelled against what we thought was unbiblical and even cult-like. We weren't used to practices that didn't conform to our American evangelical orthodoxy. In fact, I received the same reaction when I introduced it to our community back in the Philippines upon returning from the program. It felt too solemn and too Roman Catholic. None of us were used to the rituals and slowness.

We were told though that after we graduated, we should practice it in our community for a few years before sharing it with our other colleagues. It was such a struggle, to move out of a highly cognitive or cerebral spirituality into a more experiential encounter. Yet during this time, the life and teachings of St. Ignatius, Teresa of Avila and St. John of the Cross slowly began to grow inside me and our community.

Today, I strongly believe that contemplative spirituality needs to be the core of our ministry. We will not survive the exhausting work in the slums without it.

Contemplative spirituality helps us see things from a larger perspective. Instead of thinking of making a difference for ten to fifty years in the ministry, we can look towards a thousand years. This alone makes a world of difference. It changes our outlook to ministry from a sprint, to a marathon, and finally to a walk – which some people call a pilgrimage. When we use one-thousand years as our premise, everything we do changes right away.

The "Get Rich Quick" mentality of the world has so penetrated Christian ministry that projects are falling apart like industrial derelicts. We want instant gratification; we want to experience the successes of our projects right now. Everything has to be done now, completed now, within our lifetime or earlier. As a result, everything is also shallow and vain. It is the same with the world, full of fantasies and illusions.

The contemplative spirituality adjusted our pace so we don't get burnt out every five years like I was in the habit of doing. We began looking into the deepest core of spirituality—repetition. I have taught this several times to our members, and yet even now it is not easy for some to grasp. Spirituality is all about repetition, the boring and ordinary. Once we are able to embrace that, we begin to embrace true biblical spirituality. If we don't understand the slowness that comes with learning spirituality, all our efforts will lead to vanity. We cannot fill our void, and we will be addicted to sensational experiences. The world where we need to bring Christ is boring. Most of our daily activities are repetitious and ordinary—washing the dishes, changing diapers, driving the same streets. Yet, instead of teaching people to embrace the daily grind, we encourage them to seek for a high, a sort of existential need for thrill.

One of the things we learned in our program in Hong Kong was the three-day silent retreat. We've been holding these retreats now for almost 15 years, three to four times a year.

For three days and two nights we gather in a Roman Catholic monastery with strict rules. We are completely silent – no gadgets, music, exercising, communication, or books. Not even a Bible (passages from the Psalms, Old Testament, and New Testament are read three times a day, and we are given other material to read for meditation, which ends up being more than enough for our meditation and reflection in-between our times of worship and our meals).

Most evangelical retreats reinforce seeking a spiritual high, which only leads to burn-out. Silent retreats, on the other hand, make us rested, and in turn, more able to see our interior lives. It is in the retreats that we see our demons, often times things we have been avoiding for decades. We have intentionally been running around like headless chickens, busying ourselves to repress the demons inside us.

The main principle of silent retreats is, the more rested we are, the more we can hear God. Most of the time, our praying is really just us reciting what we wish for. In silent retreats, we learn the prayer of listening. This is what we want to offer to people in the slums, the peace and love of Jesus, not our restlessness and drivenness.

It is important that we practice these retreats as a community. Silent retreats are not individual affairs. Listening and waiting is a community affair. There is a big difference between praying alone and praying three times a day with fifty other people. It is a kind of cadence when we all meet together to wait and listen for the Lord. This is the core of our relationship as a community. We can thus say, we are not just a family, or a social mutual help organization, or a mission organization, or an NGO helping the poor. We are primarily a community on a pilgrimage in prayer.

9: The Role of Solitude

Spiritual journey involves solitude through silence and storytelling where we connect our small stories with the big story of God in the Bible.

Seeking solitude is an integral part in journeying with the poor. Only by finding solitude can we be at peace in the slums. Once we have sought solitude, we will be able to commune with the poor. We offer ourselves to them and also receive from them.

We journey in solitude through storytelling and silence. To seek solitude is to listen. It is through listening that we can see Christ in the sick, the dying and the hungry. Mother Teresa worked sixteen hours a day among the lepers of Calcutta, including eight hours in prayer and eight hours in the field holding the hands of the dying. The whole sixteen hours intertwined as a rhythm of contemplation and action, going in and out of the chapel like two strands in a twine.

Solitude is a spiritual exercise of attending to the presence of God. This involves a lot of silence, either alone or together in community. It takes years to master. We start to grasp it from the garden, or retreat center, a comfortable space, before we boldly and cautiously venture into tougher situations, like the desert. Once we are able to hold onto our solitude, we can finally transition into the slums.

As we work in the slums, we may lose the solitude we had carefully nurtured in the garden or in the desert. It is difficult to remain contemplative in noisy and smelly shanties. We may need to keep going back to the silence of the chapel or the garden, and with persistence we will be able to hold it. It is at this stage our journey begins to gain meaning.

What is the solitude we hold? It is the presence of Jesus. When it was near the time for Jesus to die, He told the disciples that soon they would all abandon Him and run away and He would be left alone. And yet He would not be alone, He said, because the Father would be with Him. This is the difference between aloneness and loneliness. Solitude is about aloneness, being alone with God. Loneliness is feeling cut off from God, others and even from oneself.

How do we let the slums enter into our solitude and expose our nakedness? How does our solitude fare while we live in the slums? With solitude, we learn to reach out to others from Christ, who is our center. The goal of the journey is to be able to see Christ in others, and to be able to see with the eyes of Christ. It is being able to see Christ among the poor. This was the main belief of Mother Teresa. She said she sees Christ in the sick and in the dying. When she ministers to the poor, she ministers directly to Christ. This approach requires a lot of discernment and contemplation, requiring a lot of discipline in solitude.

Our journey in the slums opens us up to our own redemption. The poverty of the slums exposes who we truly are, especially the poverty and injustice inside of us. In this way, being in the slums shows the slums inside our own hearts. Jesus learned obedience from the things he suffered. We will also learn obedience when we experience suffering in the slums.

In order to experience the presence of God, we must begin with silence. It is easy to make the outside world silent. What is hard is to make the inner world silent. Once we begin the journey to be silent inside, we start on a long and difficult journey but a fully rewarding one.

As mentioned before, one way our community learns to be silent is by going into the mountains three times a year for three-day silent retreats. We observed that three days is the minimum time to truly enter into solitude. Then, in between our retreats, we participate together in community two to three times a day in *lectio divina*, or divine reading, where we carry over the silence that we find during the retreats.

Experiencing silence however does not come simply by attending a silent prayer retreat or spending time alone. Honesty is needed in order to experience the presence of God. Many people have gone with us into the mountains and dismissed it completely. They will tell their friends that they have gone to a silent retreat and it was meaningless, all because they were not honest in their silence. During their supposed silence, they actively engaged their minds and bodies. Their bodies never slow down, and their minds wander to so many distant places. Or worse, they do sit in silence and fall asleep. Although it is good to rest a body that has been battled for years by stress and little sleep, if rest is sought to make the soul sleep, to become oblivious, then it is bad. It was not their goal to enter into the presence of Jesus at all. Silent retreats should be done because we desire to be with Jesus.

What is a bad silent retreat? It is a silent retreat conducted by leaders who are not in the habit of solitude themselves. Or it is a silent retreat that is not really silent at all (six hours of group discussion a day about silence or about meditation), because there is no one who knows how to experience true solitude. Some think they are silent because they are not speaking with their mouth, but they are not really silent because their eyes, bodies, and hands still interact, making signals or gestures. Others spend time doing exercises like jogging, calisthenics, and tai-chi, which also prevents them from truly being silent. Their mouths are silent but their bodies are not.

At first, it is normal to feel restless and uncomfortable. The silence is deafening and we cannot sit still in our seats because we're conditioned to move and be productive. It feels like we will explode because everything is so still— nothing and no one in the room moves or makes any noise. But we must remain in this tension, until we get to a place where our hearts are silent and we can experience God's presence and hear His voice. As one of the signs says upon entering the retreat center we use for our retreats, "In the silence of our hearts, the Lord speaks."

When we return to the slums after the retreat, we need to be able to remain in God's presence. In other words, even in the slums, we need to constantly quiet our hearts in order to hear His voice. This is difficult, because like in the desert, the slums are extremely uncomfortable. It is so hard to remain quiet because everything is so crowded and noisy. The poverty too can be so oppressive that one easily loses their equilibrium, and easily loses touch with God.

How then can we see Christ among the poor, the sick and the dying if we are so easily and frequently distracted? There are so many sick people, and so many little children running around shouting and playing. There are so many needs, so many hurts and pains. How do we remain calm and composed? How do we remain in the presence of God?

We need to cultivate solitude so that it can remain with us even after we have left the garden. We practice it constantly, and after many years it begins to take root in us and become like a second nature, so that even the noise and distraction of the slums cannot dislodge it.

10: Storytelling

There are the two pillars of our journey—prayer and storytelling. One pillar brings us closer to the Word and the other pillar brings us closer to each other. Both bring us closer to God together as a community.

A second pillar of our journey is storytelling. Storytelling is what binds the community together, underlying our common cause and shared journey. Stories move into our passions and desires, impelling us to live for something higher than ourselves and to go beyond the call of duty. Stories work from within. We identify with warriors, and we are swallowed up in tales of sacrifice, honor, courage and love. We are able to imagine Christ as a person and in relation to other people. This makes it easy for us to enter into the picture and become part of the story.

Jesus bound people by stories and parables. He was an expert storyteller. He was able to pierce through the *corpus callosum,* or the link between the left and right brain. The left brain is comprised of logical thinking and calculation while the right brain is susceptible to feelings and experiences. Jesus was able to connect these two sides by using both parables and stories.

A way to connect storytelling with solitude is by listening to the stories and parables of Jesus through *lectio divina*, or divine reading. We do this in our community by reading the Gospel out loud during Bible studies, worship, and silent retreats, then entering into the story through twenty minutes of silence.

I have not seen a Bible study approach more powerful than the *lectio divina*. There are many ways to do Bible studies, but *lectio divina* invites the participant to enter the story. A passage in the Gospel is chosen, usually where there is a dialogue with Jesus. It must not be too long; just one story or encounter with Jesus is enough. The text is read several times, and for each reading the reader instructs the listeners (a bunch of scavengers working in the Payatas dumpsite) how to listen.

First, they are told to listen to the reading with their bodies, to feel and sense the surroundings. Is it hot, dry, or noisy? What do they smell? Then for the second reading, they are instructed to listen with their hearts and their feelings. Is it sad, joyful, or exciting? The third may be to listen with their eyes. What do they see? Is it crowded? Are the people clean? What are they wearing? What is the expression on Jesus' face? Finally, they are asked to listen with their mind. What do they hear? What is God saying to them?

In the conclusion, each one is asked to choose or identify with one character in the story. The listener picks a character and tells the group why he or she chose that person. This approach to the Bible is revolutionary and I have seen it mightily impact the poor.

As we have journeyed with the urban poor in the Philippines over the last forty years, we have found their stories to be quite riveting. The urban poor or slum dwellers are the last people we would consider as missionaries, even though they do a great work in the harvest. Many go out as missionaries but they do not look like missionaries at all. They are construction workers, domestic helpers, nurses, and seamen; often times poor and uneducated like in the book of Acts. They are able to go to places that are impossible for other missionaries—like Saudi Arabia, or very expensive cities like Tokyo.

More than eleven-million Filipinos work overseas. If we assume that 10% are Christians, that would be 1.1 million Christians. If we say 10% of those are actively and boldly sharing the Gospel that would be a staggering 110,000 missionaries! That would make the Filipino church the largest missionary force ever mobilized into the harvest in the entire history of Christian mission. The goal of the South Korean church is to have that many missionaries in the next decade. In other words, while it is still a goal of South Korea, the Filipino church has already accomplished it. But no one bothers and no one is impressed. The poor often do not figure into the calculation of the church and missions.

The experiences of Christian OFWs (Overseas Filipino Workers) echo the actions and dynamics of the very first missionaries in the book of Acts. In both occasions, they are poor, uneducated, and were uprooted from their original environments. They were forced out either by drought, persecution, or to look for jobs. OFW missionaries do not leave for any romantic motive to share the Gospel but to earn and provide for their families back home. Evangelism is incidental or accidental in most cases.

Our pastor in the slum in Santo Domingo became a pastor in Tokyo, to an all-Filipino church. One of their members was a Japayuki (slang for Filipina entertainers in clubs). The girl's mother was our member in the Santo Domingo slum church. Slowly they ministered to local Japanese people. Their church grew in number and began sending missionaries. They even have churches now in places like Vancouver and Oregon.

The strangest thing for me is reverse mission. Some Filipinos came to know Jesus in foreign lands. They often carry the mentality that there are no born-again Christians in the Philippines. We met a *balikbayan* (a Filipino that goes abroad for any number of years, then returns to the Philippines) while mobilizing in a slum in Kaingin. She told me about her church in the Middle East, of their burden for mission, and their desire to reach her relatives here in the Philippines, right there in Kaingin. I was stunned. She actually sees her own country as a mission field. Through her church's prayers in the Middle East, I believe the church in the Kaingin slum was planted. Her family all came to know Jesus and became the first members of our church there.

Another one of our pastors, Pastora Leone, has the same reverse mission mentality. She also came to Christ while working in the Middle East and returned to be a missionary in the Philippines. Until recently, when her community was demolished and relocated, she was serving as a pastor in the slum church in Pulang Lupa. Her daily habit was to go house to house, asking permission to pray for people inside their homes. She did it regularly, although at times it didn't seem to be effective or valuable to the people she prayed for. One day, she accidentally skipped a house. Before she returned to the church, the woman in the house she skipped was already there, ready to pick a fight with her for skipping her house. Apparently, everyone was already expecting her rounds and were deeply impacted by her prayers.

Stories from Scripture and our own contexts move us to a higher plane; they make us live not just for ourselves but also for an ideal. When we live for something higher, we become more than mortals. We become nobles, warriors, fearless heroes and heroines. Death no longer seems terrifying and life becomes more enticing. Some of our prayers are weird or funny, but they only add to the strange ways in which miracles take place. Without our stories, the community will quickly degenerate into a social club or a charitable organization. The movement and dynamism of community remains alive primarily through storytelling.

11: Liturgy

Obey these instructions as a lasting ordinance for you and your descendants. When you enter the land that the Lord will give you as he promised, observe this ceremony. And when your children ask you, "What does this ceremony mean to you?" tell them... – Exodus 12:24-27

How do we make our churches last a thousand years? Most churches, according to scientific surveys, last only ten years at most. Most services are structured like secular programs: always thrill seeking and emotional, if not too intellectual. It feeds the human desire for something new and avoids at all costs repetitions because these become tedious and tiresome to endure.

The Church is said to be composed of three things: worship, mission, and community. These three are tied together by liturgy. During the liturgy, superiority melts away. There is no leader, no big shot. Everyone humbles and empties himself to bow down to God. The Psalmist says, "God dwells in the worship (or liturgy) of His people" (Psalm 22:3). This is the way to build community. Liturgy allows the spirit of the group to unite as the Body of Christ.

A church will last a thousand years with the practice of liturgy. It infuses a sense of mystery into church life and worship. When we look that far, all our presuppositions and values change. When we simply look at the next ten years or more, we become very nearsighted and earthbound.

Mystery as used in the Bible does not mean we have a secret formula or secret knowledge that makes us more superior than others. Something is a mystery simply because one has not known Jesus. The secrets in the biblical mysteries are actually open secrets but open only to those who have a personal knowledge of Jesus.

Liturgy then, acknowledges God's entire being as a mystery to us, and often illuminates His hidden meanings. The liturgy carries us through times when we have lost our desire for God. The rich symbolism of liturgy also helps us to see God beyond our intellect and reason.

Mystery is distinguished from rational things in that rational things are apprehended by the mind but mysteries are apprehended by the spirit. The way to know the unknowable is through symbols and rituals that provide expressions that go beyond words and reason. When we confine worshipers to merely cognitive processes, we actually limit their knowledge of God.

Many Christian groups conduct their fellowships with a short spontaneous prayer and some loud singing before the sermon. The sermon is believed to be the most important part of the service, and the other parts are just ancillary. However, for a good liturgical worship service, the people need to arrive half an hour early to collect themselves. They sit down and quiet themselves, calming their spirits from the hustle of the travel to the venue. They anticipate the worship and take time to make themselves present. People think they only need their minds while in fellowship. Since the most important thing is the sermon, they only need to pay attention to what the pastor is saying, without needing their hearts and bodies.

In Companion With the Poor, we believe that the more rested we are, the more we can hear God. Our bodies play a big part in our spirituality. We are careful to listen to God in silence so we can petition more effectively. We find it dangerous that we may be raising petitions of our own wills rather than God's will.

One of the elements of liturgy is the profound sense of sacredness in the ordinary. Our spirituality is borne out of the ordinary, repetitious, and boring. People don't really understand this, so they mistake new and exciting things as spirituality. It makes them detached from the ordinary. We should be able to see the sacred in the ordinary. This is in contrast with man's frequent addiction for things that are new, special, sensational and extravagant. Searching for God and being grateful both for the ordinary and the spectacular allows the Christian community to last and grow together, even for a thousand years. It is a life of solitude and seeking, finding beauty in the humdrum and unspectacular in order to achieve peace of self.

Those whose tasks take longer than others understand the sacredness in the ordinary better than others. The farmer plants a tree that will take years before it bears fruit. The fisherman waits a long time to catch a fish. A mother who prepares meals for her family experiences the repetition of ordinary things daily. Washing the dishes over and over again is also ordinary, and even boring. This is our reality and our spirituality must be attached to it in order to have meaning, and in order to impact our lives. Spirituality that is borne of addiction to new and exciting things will tend to make people zoom out of reality and become irrelevant to life.

The liturgy is also a reminder that seeking God is a journey, comprised of repetitious, ordinary disciplines, and not a one-time encounter. Our sense of a spiritual journey forms part of the liturgy—our being present, our anticipation, and our solitude as we listen to God. By looking at the next one thousand years, this journey becomes a slow walk, a pilgrimage. Spirituality is thus not a sprint, and not even a marathon. It grows like the leaves on the tree, slowly, and imperceptibly.

Our journey is most aptly described in the story of the Road to Emmaus. It had only been three days since the death of Jesus, and everyone in the town had heard of the news. Two of His disciples were walking on the road when Jesus joined them. They talked while walking together, but the disciples did not recognize that it was their Lord they were talking to. After some time, it began to grow dark so the disciples invited Jesus for the night. At the dinner table, Jesus broke the bread and it was only then that their eyes were opened and they recognized that it was their Lord. Then, in the blink of an eye, Jesus disappeared.

This story represents our journey and liturgy—Jesus appearing and disappearing. It is a journey through life with Jesus as our companion, although He isn't always visible or present. When He does appear, He could disappear as suddenly as He appeared.

The hard part is when He does not appear. Sometimes we spend days in solitude, but we're stranded in a spiritual desert. When this happens, our longings must grow. One French poet wrote that being apart from loved ones kills the small flames but fans the big flames to grow. When God does not appear, the bigger flame of our longing must burst out and grow. It is not true that if we do things right, liturgy will guarantee His presence. Sometimes, when we do it right, and when we have done all we can, His presence seems to intentionally become out of our reach. He does not appear. As Teresa of Avila warned long ago, many fall in love with their spirituality but not Jesus. Their own spirituality becomes the main obstacle to finding God.

The scene of Jesus on the cross is the utmost example of crying out to God. Jesus implored, "God why have you forsaken me?" After this cry, He obeyed all of God's commands, even the supreme command of being nailed to the cross for the sins of mankind. This is the deepest mystery of all; that God seems to abandon us at the moment we cry for Him. Liturgy is simply not a guarantee He will be there; or as it says in the teachings of St. John of the Cross, we may think he is not there when in fact he is (the Psalmist says, *God is engulfed by dark clouds*). (Psalm 18:11) He said, as we mature, things seem to turn upside down and what is light is actually dark and what is dark is actually the true light of God. During that period, we may enter what he calls the dark nights of the soul.

Liturgy in the end is simply an acknowledgement of that sacred space inside all of us, where from time to time, God would appear. Though we cannot force Him, He invites us constantly; it is He who constantly calls, "Come."

Today many are ignorant of the profound symbolisms in the liturgy because no one explained it to them. We eventually forget. The liturgy soon loses its meaning. The next generation will not understand, and they will begin to say that the liturgy or worship is irrelevant. So our task really is to continually teach and explain its meaning, telling them why we are doing it and then to revive its drama.

The liturgy is a very useful tool in worshiping together. It is a personal and collective encounter of Christ, and the fellowship of the community through intense and emotional spiritual mountains, as well as through the desert when God seems to be silent. The liturgy is what builds, cultivates and expands the community. It welcomes new believers into the family and treats them as new brothers and sisters. It takes so much effort and consensus for a group to come together in silence or in prayer. To agree to wait on God together is a miracle already. Prayer is not all about talking and talking. Praying is mostly about listening to God, waiting and desiring. The corporate act of praying thus is where we supremely make Christ concrete in our midst.

Reflections on *Solitude* from CWTP Missionaries

The styles of our worship and liturgy are completely different from what I'm used to. I grew up a Pentecostal, so I am used to noisy and energy-filled services. This is a new experience in terms of worship. I can feel God's presence through the silence; it's very difficult to explain. Prior to my participation in this type of worship, I thought one would be able to feel God through tension, through the volume of music, but here you will feel God in music that you can't hear. – Jhe R

I learned to live quieter and to experience the presence of the Lord. [The liturgy] has greatly contributed to my personal walk with God.
– Banjo

At first, I was a bit startled because [the liturgy] wasn't familiar to me. I came from the Assemblies of God, where their worship is quite different. It's noisier. I thought, how am I supposed to feel the movement of the Holy Spirit through this! But now, I enjoy our worship, and I think it's very beautiful. – Irene

The work in the slums isn't easy. We need a contemplative perspective so we can be able to see Christ in one another, in the poor and in our spouse.
– Raineer

Of course, when [the liturgy] was still new, it was a different experience for all of us. But through time, it sort of became life, you know? It became breath. *[Because we've been practicing this for some time now], I deeply appreciate silence and listening. – Jojo*

The liturgy is what guides us back when we stray off from the Lord. It's the pattern to return to God. It keeps your walk with the Lord consistent. The liturgy is very important to us. We've

decided to make it part of our lives until we die. – Moises

I enjoy the liturgy because I can really feel the presence of the Lord.
– Sonny

CWTP is serious about finding God and listening to His word.
– Hadassa

By nature, I tend to be an activist and a social reformer. I enjoy filling my days with new, exciting and proactive innovative activities. The liturgy of CWTP enables me to slow down, empowers me to keep still and know that I am not God, and equips me to listen to the Lord and to my soul and body. I fight not to miss our quarterly silent retreat where for three days we keep still and know that God is God. – Corrie

My first experience in liturgy was really difficult, but now it's wonderful to be silent and listen to the presence of the Holy Spirit in my life, especially in the reading of the Word  *of God. I've been blessed in the liturgy. – Marivic*

 *I've learned a lot from CWTP for the last 5 years. I learned to slow down and be silent before the Lord. I learned to be open and humble myself before the Lord. Knowing that I can't do anything without Him, I have learned to be dependent on Him all the time. – Nehemias*

Fifteen years ago, I did not like the lectio or the silence. Maybe because I was used to pray and worship God in a louder voice. As the years have gone by, I have learned to appreciate it. And the silence became my rest. I also like the hugging and the hand shaking of the missionaries at the end of our worship time. – Mary Ann

[Our liturgy] is very deep and genuine! We can meet the Lord, and truly worship Him as individuals and as a community. – Nesie

Our liturgy has provided me with a good tool for listening to the voice of God through silence. I enjoy it very much. It is a way of praying that does not simply allow us to utter prayers, but encourages us to listen to and encounter God through silence and waiting upon him. – Reggie

Our liturgy is a guide for how we can get closer to God, ask for forgiveness, receive His grace and be with God in remembering the Holy Communion. In liturgy, unity is built. There is forgiveness, greetings, shaking of hands and praying for each other. It's not always easy to associate with one another, but through liturgy, we are led to have peace (shalom) with one another and with God. – Dan

In our retreats, I am able to gain new strength for my ministry, and to be refreshed in my heart, body, mind, and soul. The Scriptures that are read and the times of silence encourage me and challenge me to continue in my ministry and relationship with the Lord. – Godjell

Because of our lectio divina, I have been able to encounter God in my everyday life. I feel happy and blessed, and it really feels good every time I do the lectio divina. Through lectio divina, I am able to find rest not just for my physical body but also from within. And whenever I read God's word and humble myself in silence, God enables me to feel His presence, see His glory and hear His voice. Through these things, I feel more thirsty and hungry for His presence in my life. – Ederlyn

Epilogue: Building a Religious Community

The family is our refuge and our springboard; nourished on it, we can advance to new horizons. In every conceivable manner, the family is the link to our past, and the bridge to our future. – Alex Haley

We are trying to build Companion With the Poor into a religious community, rather than simply a mission organization. First, we are trying to imitate the models of societies of celibate priests and nuns, though in CWTP we are mostly all married and have lots of children.

What we have is an open and inclusive society: males and females, both married and single. Perhaps it will be easier to just move towards becoming a religious society in stages. If we imagine our group being only the members, it seems manageable. The next step would be how to get the spouses and kids into the picture. But for now, we are simply just trying to work with a blend of male and female staff (as though none were married or have kids).

At this time in our journey, we also have to ensure that our community is financially sustainable, meaning we can take care of our staff's basic needs—housing, food, transportation and education. This is the meaning of Deuteronomy 15:4 that there were no poor among them.

In Acts 4, verses 32-35, it says,

> All the believers were one in heart and mind. No one claimed that any of their possessions was their own, but they shared everything they had. With great power the apostles continued to testify to the resurrection of the Lord Jesus. And God's grace was so powerfully at work in them all that there were no needy persons among them. For from time to time those who owned land or houses sold them, brought the money from the sales and put it at the apostles' feet, and it was distributed to anyone who had need.

The Apostle Paul also taught the Corinthians this principle: he who gathered much did not have too much and he who gathered little did not lack anything. In our society, it would mean an equitable financial or economic sharing of wealth.

I believe we have reached that point. We have applied the Marxist maxim, "To him who has much, much is required, and to him whose need is great, much is also given." It is not equality, but equity.

As we move into the second stage, we are now considering housing for the missionaries' families. This becomes more expensive. We are moving fast in this direction, providing for all our senior staff and their families.

The other consideration in this stage is the education of the children. Primary and secondary education is free, and now public college education has become free. For those desiring private education, we are able to provide our children with scholarships. Many have already graduated.

We have tried to redirect our finances to establish an across the board support for all staff in terms of SSS (Social Security), Philhealth (Health Insurance), and Pag-Ibig (Mortgage Loan), and we have reached that in a way, at least for a couple of years already.

When we speak of a society, we are looking both at spiritual discipline, as well as economic arrangement. Two of our leaders, Pastor Leo and Pastor Winston, are working out the spiritual disciplines, and we have more or less a modicum of an ideal economic arrangement.

There are still many obstacles. The spouses are far from the rhythm of spiritual exercises that we desire, mostly because they are homemakers or working abroad. Even more though, the kids are probably the biggest challenge. This is almost like building Noah's ark. We won't know if our ark will float at all when the water rises. What happens if these kids do not become believers?

This is a journey and we need to discern God's timing. Perhaps, God wants it to take us forty years to travel a distance that normally would take only a couple of years.

We have a strong leadership as well. I believe that we have the kind of people who can take us forward into the future, into a religious society. We have set the true foundation of the society already, which is the sense of equality. When we vote, both the missionary and his or her spouse votes. Very few groups want to implement the one-man one-vote concept in the organization; but in doing so, we have given the power to all of our members.

We also are a people-driven group. Some NGOs or societies are either fund-driven or program-driven. An example of program-driven societies are the microfinance or the family planning groups. A fund-driven group is like the USAID; when the funds are gone, their work stops. As a people-driven group, when the funds are gone, we still continue. In fact, we have always worked practically without funds. Our main capital is people who have a strong motivation and commitment and will not resign when there is no salary.

We have also developed a culture of a family. This is perhaps the biggest asset we have. People here feel like this is their family. Our members borrow money just to attend our worship or prayer meetings. Most groups treat their people as mere staff and have a culture that is corporate, like in the business world. Recognizing that the biblical model is very difficult, it can feel at times like an uphill climb. But it helps to see it as a journey, a journey of a thousand years.

I have walked that long road to freedom. I have tried not to falter; I have made missteps along the way. But I have discovered the secret that after climbing a great hill, one only finds that there are many more hills to climb. I have taken a moment here to rest, to steal a view of the glorious vista that surrounds me, to look back on the distance I have come. But I can only rest for a moment, for with freedom come responsibilities, and I dare not linger, for my long walk is not ended. - Nelson Mandela

Questions for Discussion

To help facilitate a small group discussion for each chapter, a quote and Scripture passage has been provided for each chapter. Supplemental Scripture passages are also included. One potential structure for discussion is as follows:

Opening Prayer

Read the Chapter & Quote

Answer Discussion Questions

Read the Scripture (x 2)

5-10 minutes Silence

Discuss the Scripture

Read/Discuss Supplemental Scriptures if time allows

Closing Prayer

Preface: Finding our Freedom

Quote for Reflection (p. 11): "The Apostle Paul said, "I know what it is to live in plenty and I know what it is to live in want" (Philippians 4:11). When we are bound by our material possessions, we have no freedom. As Christians, we must be able to say that even without our laptop or cell phone, we will survive. I can enjoy the lavish life of the wealthy but I also will not be crippled when cast into utter poverty."

Do you know what it is like to live in plenty and to live in want? What does this have to do with our spirituality and Christian journey?

Main Scripture: Luke 12:13-34

Additional Scripture: Job 2:9-10, Matthew 6:19-24, Matthew 6:25-34, Philippians 4:10-13

Introduction

Quote for Reflection (p. 14): "God has no miraculous agenda to get rid of the poverty in the world at large. His agenda, following a structure taught by the Bible, is to get rid of poverty in the church. This is why the church is called the "contrast society". It is a counter-cultural community composed of believers who demonstrate living in the kingdom as the ideal life of shalom under the Lordship of God. One manifestation of this is that in the church there is no more poor. The social action to alleviate poverty must begin within the church as proof that our gospel works. It can overflow to the world at large but only after it has been shown to work within."

What does it look like to be a "counter-cultural community"? How is your Christian community different from other communities in the world around you? What could your community do to better care for the poor among you?

Main Scripture: Deuteronomy 15:1-11

Additional Scripture: Philippians 2:1-11, James 2:14-17

Chapter 1: Begin with Community

Quote for Reflection (p. 21): "In addition to our disciplines, we encourage our missionaries to balance their work, ministry, family, and brokenness; and to live by faith and raise support. We raise support as a way of developing humility. We also engage in livelihood activities (part-time work) to augment our support. Married people are taught to make their marriage and families a higher priority than serving in the ministry. We welcome broken people to serve as wounded healers. We believe that we all came from a bad past until Christ saved us. We also believe we are all works in progress, which is precisely why we say we are on a journey. We have found Jesus but we also continue to look for Him. We have been saved fully and finally but we also continue to seek His salvation daily. We have absolute assurance of our salvation but we also tremble and doubt our salvation."

Have you found Jesus? Are you still looking for Him? Or like with CWTP, is it both? What does it look like to journey with Jesus and the church and others in this way? How does it influence how we evangelize non-Christians?

Main Scripture: Acts 2:42-47, 4:32-37

Additional Scripture: Ecclesiastes 4:9-12, Matthew 12:46-50, Acts 2:1-21

Chapter 2: The Living Gospel

Quote for Reflection (p. 24): "The Gospel is God's call to all the nations to watch and observe His people and see God's goodness. His people should be living examples of blessings and prosperity who share to the less fortunate. They don't ignore their poorer Christian brothers and sisters. Instead, they feed, clothe and take care of the poor and needy in their midst. When they have conflicts, they forgive and reconcile. The living Gospel is preached as an invitation for unbelievers to desire to become part of the community of God."

Is this a good description of your community or church? Are the rich and poor separated in your church and/or community? What steps can your church take to be a better representation of the living gospel talked about in this chapter?

Main Scripture: Revelation 2:8-11, 3:14-22

Additional Scripture: Genesis 17:1-8, 2 Chronicles 17:1-10, Ezekiel 37:1-14, Matthew 5:13-16, Matthew 28:16-20, John 6:60-71, John 14:25-31, Acts 8:26-39, 2 Corinthians 3:1-6

Chapter 3: Holding all Things in Common

Quote for Reflection (p. 31): "The church that has given away everything can say to the beggar, *Silver and gold I have none but this I say unto you, arise in the name of Christ* (Acts 3:6). Giving our all is true wealth. But who will listen to that? Wealth in this world, even among Christians, is defined as hoarding, accumulating and amassing. It is keeping a bank account enough to sustain a certain "lifestyle', to afford expensive things and important friends. The biblical definition of wealth is in contrast to the lifestyles that the rich have to uphold because of their social status. Wealth is about giving. It is about how much we give instead of how much we have kept or amass. It is about how much we have blessed instead of how much we have kept for ourselves."

How do you define wealth? How does the Bible define wealth? How would your life look different if you understood wealth in this way?

Main Scripture: 2 Corinthians 8:1-15

Additional Scripture: Exodus 16:1-26, Malachi 3:6-12, Mark 10:17-31, Luke 21:1-4, 1 Corinthians 13:3, 2 Corinthians 9:6-15

Chapter 4: Journeying With the Poor

Quote for Reflection (p. 51): "When we journey with the poor, it is to find out how they live. We remove our gaze from a higher social or economic class. We try to relate to them and understand their spirituality. When we do immersion, we experience the miserable conditions that are considered normal by more than a third of the world's population. Those who 'immerse' choose to live among the poor with the intention of learning how to journey with the poor. We seek to enter into their lives and find out how they understand and express their faith and spirituality. It is far more important to learn to journey with the poor than to promote so-called development work. We must first understand why God said the poor are rich in faith. What is important is being able to see Jesus in the poor, the dying, and in the sick. Helping the poor rise out of poverty is only secondary."

Have you spent time immersing with the poor? Or even living with the poor for any amount of time? What was this experience like and what did you learn? Were you trying to understand why the poor are rich in faith? Were you able to see Jesus in the poor, the dying, and the sick? Do you agree that this should come before doing "so-called development work"?

Main Scripture: Matthew 25:31-46

Additional Scripture: Nehemiah 2:11-20, Psalm 102:15-22, Matthew 19:16-30, Mark 2:13-17, Luke 4:16-30, Luke 9:57-58, Luke 10:1-12, Luke 19:1-10, John 12:23-26, Acts 4:32-37, 1 Corinthians 9:15-23, Philippians 2:1-11

Chapter 5: Reading the Bible from the Bottom-up

Quote for Reflection (p. 57): "It is important to read the Bible from the perspective of poverty and weakness. About 90% of Christians around the world are poor. Reading the Bible from the bottom-up results in a Gospel that will produce hermeneutics that benefit the poor, instead of sanctifying their oppression. Theology has always been written from the 10% that owns 90% of the world's wealth. For that matter, their theology will never question the serious inequality of the status quo that has marginalized 90% of the world. Learning to read the Bible from the bottom-up will result in theology being drawn from below, from the perspective of the majority. It is uncanny that the Bible, which is a book for the poor, should be controlled and interpreted by the dominant few and sometimes used to oppress the majority who are poor."

Were you taught to read the Bible from the bottom-up, from the perspective of the poor and weak, or from the top-down, from the perspective of the rich and powerful? How does this perspective (one way or the other), effect how we read the Scriptures? What are some other examples (in addition to Mark 12:41-44) that might be read differently if we read it from the bottom-up?

Main Scripture: Mark 12:38-44

Additional Scripture: Isaiah 2:6-22, Matthew 19:16-30, Luke 1:46-55, Luke 6:17-26, Luke 16:19-31, 1 Corinthians 1:26-31, James 1:9-12, James 2:1-7

Chapter 6: Cultivating Fortitude

Quote for Reflection (p. 65): "When the thrill of our spiritual mountains is absent, we need to cultivate fortitude. Fortitude is staying steadfast and courageous despite pain. This is something we develop through years of obedience and humility—our experiences of highs and lows make our faith resilient. Whatever happens, we must be faithful. This is an inner strength that will not succumb to sin despite our doubts about God. Ceaseless prayer is also important. Despite our doubts, spiritual deserts, and moments when we think God is absent, our honest and raw prayers must persevere."

Are you still a new Christian or an old, experienced Christian? Is your relationship with God more like an exhilarating rollercoaster, or a slow and steady pilgrimage? How do we cultivate fortitude? What experiences in your life have helped you "grow up" and mature the most? In what areas do you still need to grow in obedience and humility?

Main Scripture: Hebrews 10:32-39

Additional Scripture: Genesis 50:19-21, Psalm 23, Psalm 27:1-14, Jeremiah 1:4-10, John 3:1-15, Acts 9:1-19, Romans 12:1-8, Galatians 5:13-26, Philippians 1:27-30, Colossians 3:1-17, 2 Timothy 1:3-14, Hebrews 11:1-40, Hebrews 12:1-17, James 1:2-18, 1 Peter 2:1-12, 1 Peter 4:12-19, 1 John 4:1-6, Jude 1:17-23, Jude 1:24-25

Chapter 7: Companions With the Poor

Quote for Reflection (p. 70): "I was so shocked! If there was a single moment in my life where I was so sure God was talking to me, it was that time. I asked the young man what his name was, and he said, "My name is Nicodemus." I almost cried. My depression lifted immediately; even the scenery didn't seem as harsh. Before, I was blinded by the dust and smell of the garbage; but now, I could see Jesus walking through the garbage, looking for Nicodemus. From there I recalled Jesus saying, "Where I am, there my servants will be" (John 12:26). I knew then that mission meant to be where Jesus was. And if Jesus were in the dumpsite, I would go there to be with him."

Has there ever been a time when you were "awakened" from a depression or time of feeling down in your life, faith, or ministry? What was that experience like? If Jesus were in human form today, where do you think he would be? Would it not make sense that if we want to be with Jesus, we would also go to where he would be?

Main Scripture: Acts 3:1-10

Additional Scripture: 2 Chronicles 17:7-9, Psalm 138:3-8, Matthew 5:1-16, Matthew 19:29-30, Luke 9:57-10:12, John 4:1-26, Acts 6:8-15, Acts 7:54-60, Acts 13:1-3, Acts 16:23-24, Romans 11:1-6, James 1:27, Revelation 7:9-12

Chapter 8: Finding our Solitude

Quote for Reflection (p. 88): "It is important that we practice these retreats as a community. Silent retreats are not individual affairs. Listening and waiting is a community affair. There is a big difference between praying alone and praying three times a day with fifty other people. It is a kind of cadence when we all meet together to wait and listen for the Lord. This is the core of our relationship as a community. We can thus say, we are not just a family, or a social mutual help organization, or a mission organization, or an NGO helping the poor. We are primarily a community on a pilgrimage in prayer."

Have you been on a silent retreat, or retreat of any kind? What was it like? Do you feel like it was a time of rest, or were you more exhausted afterwards? Were you alone, or with a group of people? Is this idea of a silent retreat (if it is new for you), something you are interested in doing or looking into? Why or why not?

Main Scripture: Luke 22:39-46

Additional Scripture: Genesis 32:24-32, Exodus 3:1-6, Exodus 8:27, Exodus 13:17-22, Exodus 19:1-3, Deuteronomy 27:9-10, 1 Samuel 3:1-21, 2 Samuel 22:7, 1 Kings 19:1-18, 2 Chronicles 7:1-3, Psalm 5:7, Psalm 27:4-14, Psalm 29:3-11, Psalm 62:1-12, Psalm 139:23-24, Isaiah 6:1-8, Daniel 9:1-3, Jonah 2:1-10, Habakkuk 2:20, Matthew 14:23, Luke 4:1-13

Chapter 9: The Role of Solitude

Quote for Reflection (p. 90): "How do we let the slums enter into our solitude and expose our nakedness? How does our solitude fare while we live in the slums? With solitude, we learn to reach out to others from Christ, who is our center. The goal of the journey is to be able to see Christ in others, and to be able to see with the eyes of Christ. It is being able to see Christ among the poor. This was the main belief of Mother Teresa. She said she sees Christ in the sick and in the dying. When she ministers to the poor, she ministers directly to Christ. This approach requires a lot of discernment and contemplation, requiring a lot of discipline in solitude."

How do we let the slums (or poverty, difficulties, and challenges) enter into our solitude and expose our nakedness? How does our solitude fare while we live in the slums (or experience challenges, poverty, and weakness)? What, according to this quote and chapter, is the goal of solitude? How do we cultivate new "lenses" to see Christ in the sick, the dying and the poor?

Main Scripture: Isaiah 58:1-14

Additional Scripture: Genesis 2:25, Deuteronomy 8:1-20, Psalm 4:7-8, Ecclesiastes 3:1-14, Lamentations 3:1-41, Mark 5:1-20, Luke 6:12-16, Luke 9:18-20, Luke 10:38-42, Luke 11:1, John 8:29, John 16:32, Hebrews 4:1-13

Chapter 10: Storytelling

Quote for Reflection (p. 99): "Stories from Scripture and our own contexts move us to a higher plane; they make us live not just for ourselves but also for an ideal. When we live for something higher, we become more than mortals. We become nobles, warriors, fearless heroes and heroines. Death no longer seems terrifying and life becomes more enticing. Some of our prayers are weird or funny, but they only add to the strange ways in which miracles take place. Without our stories, the community will quickly degenerate into a social club or a charitable organization. The movement and dynamism of community remains alive primarily through storytelling."

What are the stories that are shared and told over and over in your community? What are your favorite stories in the Scriptures? Why are stories important for community? What are some stories that aren't told in your community or church that maybe could be to strengthen the people toward God's mission in the world? How are stories related to solitude?

Main Scripture: Nehemiah 8:1-18

Additional Scripture: 2 Chronicles 17:7-9, Hosea 12:10, Matthew 13:1-23, Mark 4:1-20, Mark 12:1-12, Luke 8:9-10, John 5:39-47, John 20:30-31, John 21:25, Acts 4:13, Acts 8:1-4, Acts 11:19-26, Acts 20:7-12

Chapter 11: Liturgy

Quote for Reflection (p. 106): "The liturgy is a very useful tool in worshiping together. It is a personal and collective encounter of Christ, and the fellowship of the community through intense and emotional spiritual mountains, as well as through the desert when God seems to be silent. The liturgy is what builds, cultivates and expands the community. It welcomes new believers into the family and treats them as new brothers and sisters. It takes so much effort and consensus for a group to come together in silence or in prayer. To agree to wait on God together is a miracle already. Prayer is not all about talking and talking. Praying is mostly about listening to God, waiting and desiring. The corporate act of praying thus is where we supremely make Christ concrete in our midst."

What is the liturgy in your church, group, or Bible study? In other words, what is your order of worship, what symbols do you use, and what values or disciplines guide your group, community, or church? What about your family? What is your family's liturgy or routines during the day and during the week? How does our liturgy shape us? How can we better shape our liturgy via the Scriptures and Christian community, rather than the routines that the world tends to convince us of or impose on us?

Main Scripture: Luke 24:13-34

Additional Scripture: Exodus 12:24-27, 2 Chronicles 29:25-30, Psalm 18:11, Psalm 48:9-14, Psalm 65:1-13, Psalm 119:164, Daniel 6:10, Matthew 6:5-15, Matthew 6:16-18, Matthew 27:45-54, Mark 12:28-31, 1 Corinthians 14:26-33, Ephesians 5:15-20, 1 Thessalonians 4:1-12, 1 Timothy 2:1-15 (MSG), Revelation 22:17

Epilogue: Building a Religious Community

Quote for Reflection (p. 118): "We also are a people-driven group. Some NGOs or societies are either fund-driven or program-driven. An example of program-driven societies are the microfinance or the family planning groups. A fund-driven group is like the USAID; when the funds are gone, their work stops. As a people-driven group, when the funds are gone, we still continue. In fact, we have always worked practically without funds. Our main capital is people who have a strong motivation and commitment and will not resign when there is no salary."

Does your community or group put more emphasis on people, funds, or programs? If any of the three of these stopped for one reason or another, how would it impact your group or organization? What are some ways you can bring more balance to your group or organization, and how would you make this happen?

Main Scripture: 1 Corinthians 12:12–13:3

Additional Scripture: Genesis 6:11-22, Exodus 16:13-26, Psalm 133:1-3, Galatians 2:10

66050495R00081

Made in the USA
Columbia, SC
16 July 2019